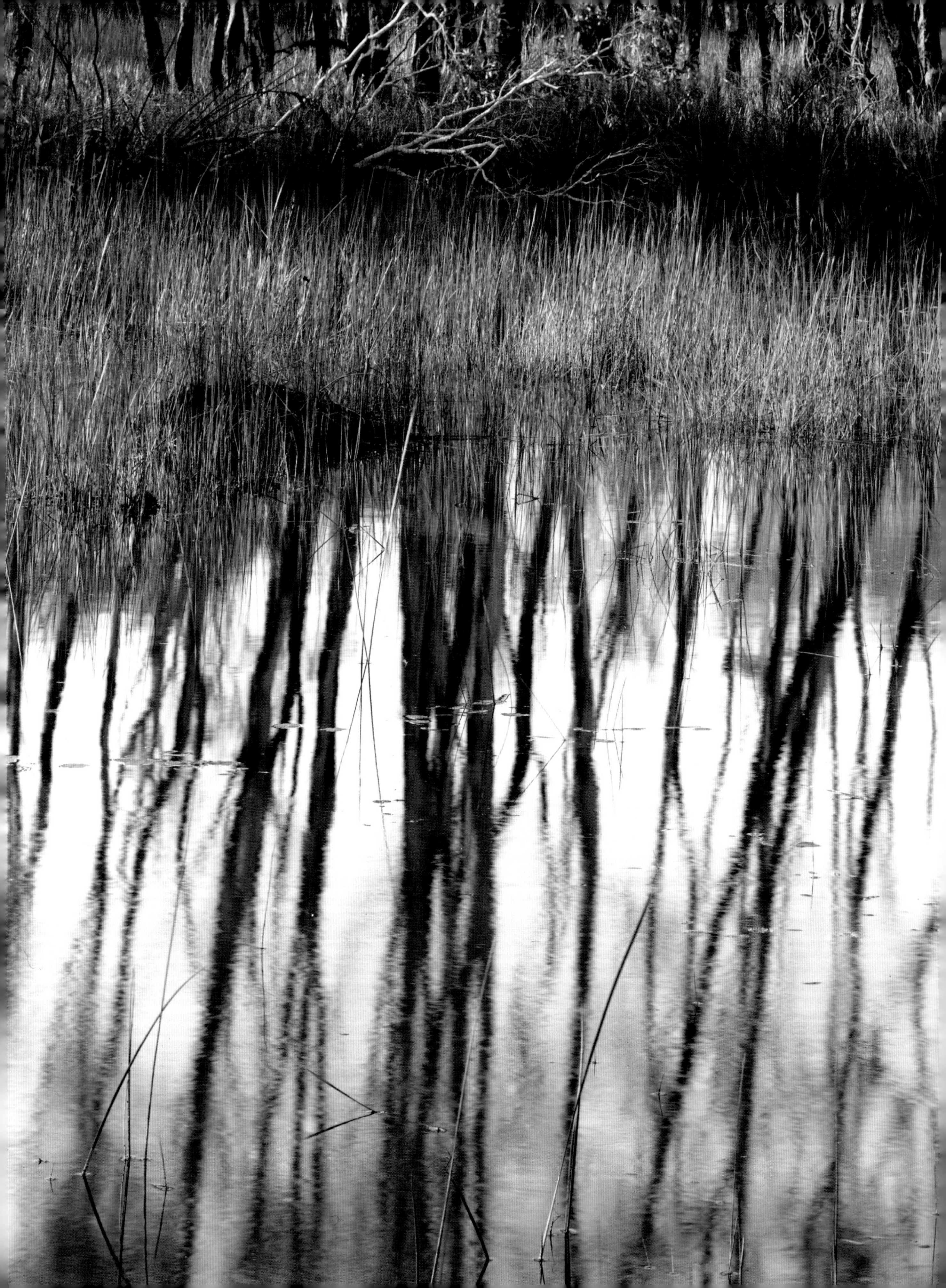

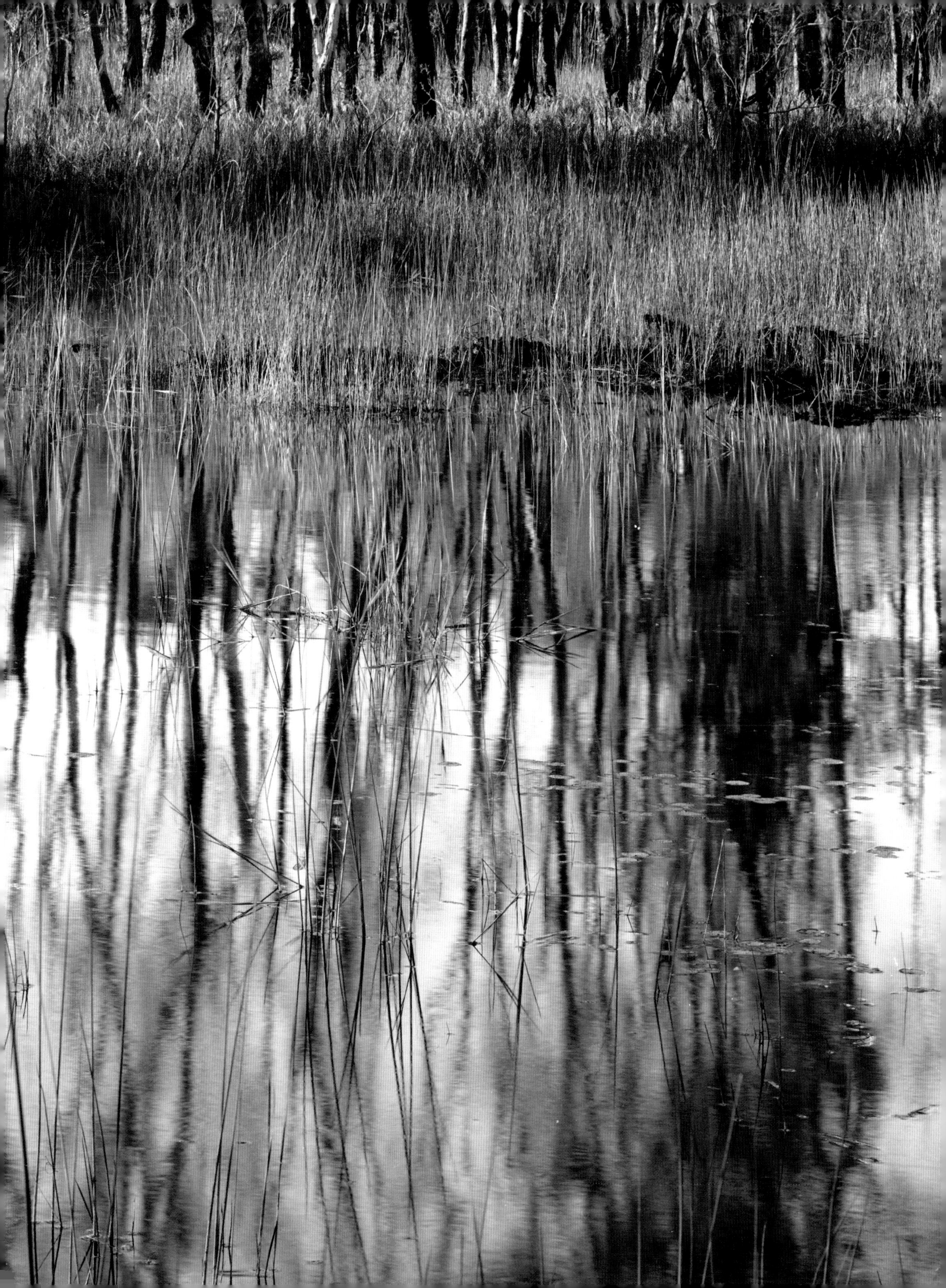

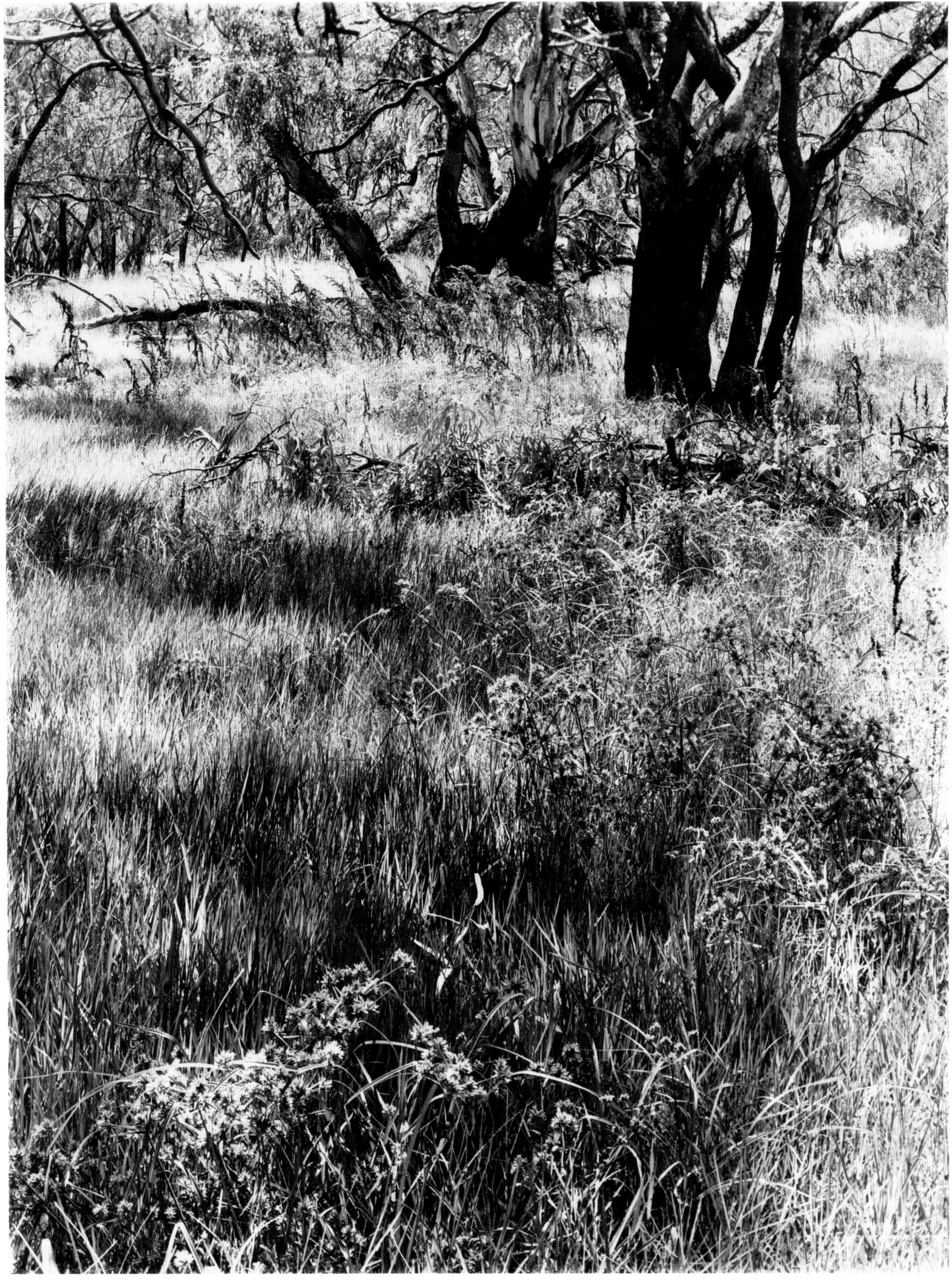

PLEASURE OF PLACE

PHOTOGRAPHS BY RICHARD STRINGER

QUEENSLAND ART GALLERY | GALLERY OF MODERN ART

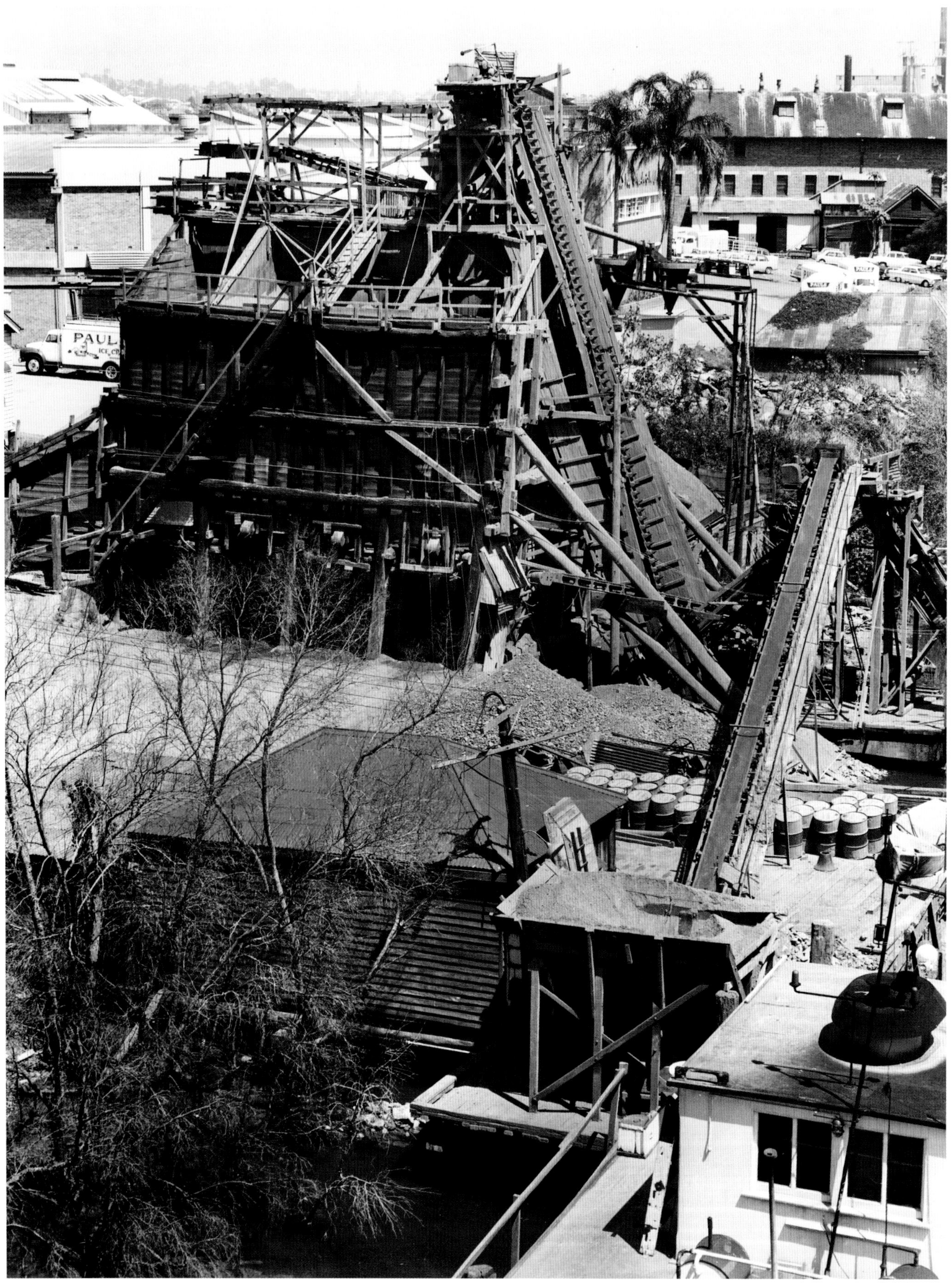

CONTENTS

Gravel deliveries, South Brisbane 1967, printed 2013

Page 4: *Billabong Creek, Jerilderie* 1986, printed 1987

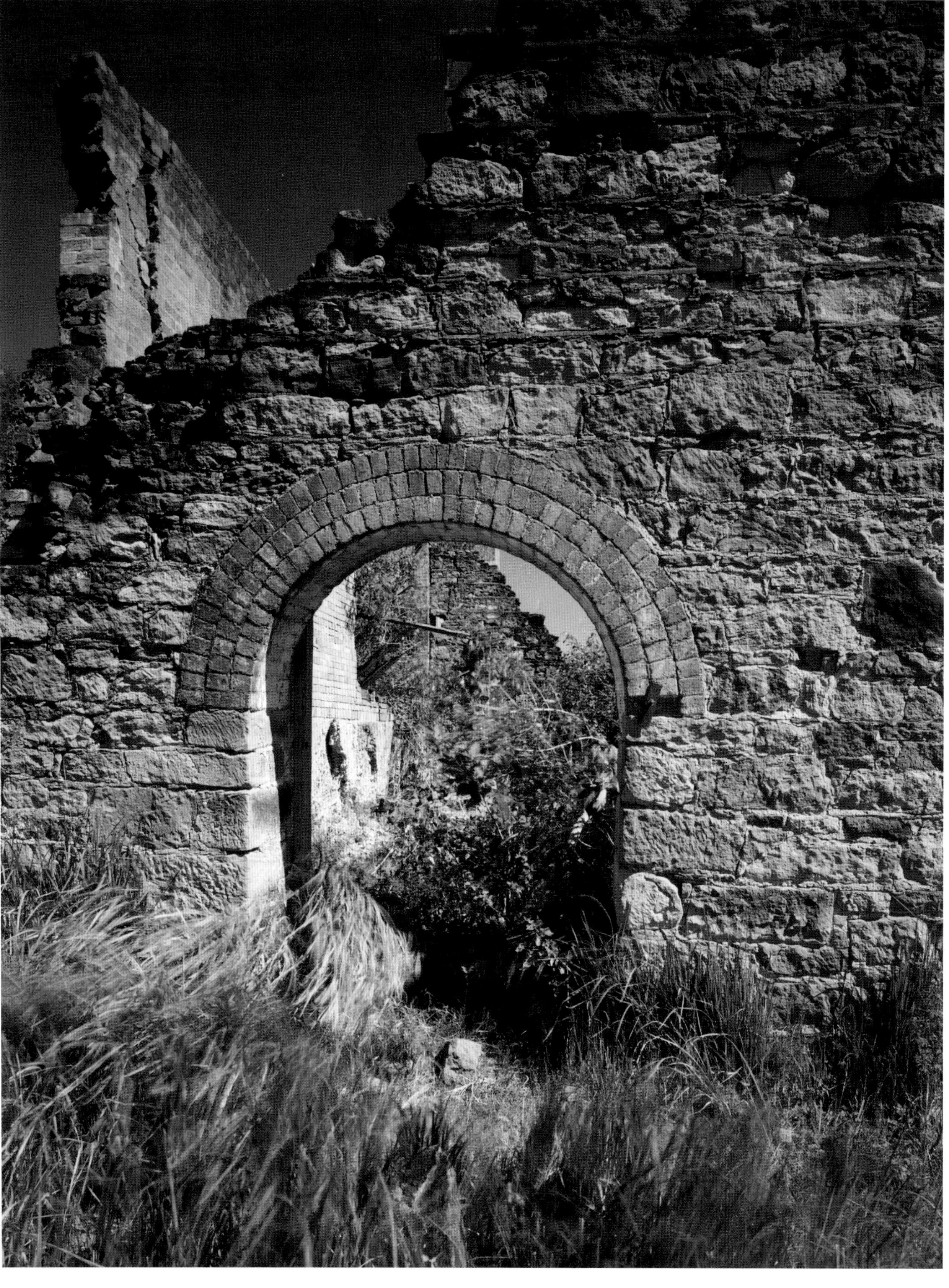

SPONSOR MESSAGE

Glencore Xstrata

Glencore Xstrata (formerly Xstrata Coal) is delighted to continue our commitment to the Queensland Art Gallery | Gallery of Modern Art through the sponsorship of the Queensland Artists' Gallery and the Regional Queensland Touring Workshop Program.

Our partnership with the Gallery forms an important part of a Corporate Social Involvement (CSI) program through which Glencore Xstrata supports initiatives in the communities in which we operate. This year, through our CSI program, we have committed $3 million to community partnerships across Queensland. Through these partnerships, we are seeing positive changes in many areas, such as health and education, social welfare and cultural development.

'Pleasure of Place: Photographs by Richard Stringer' chronicles the enduring photographic career of one of Queensland's most well-known and respected artists. Through Richard Stringer's astute eye for detail, we witness Queensland's regional history and evolving urban environment — a perfect exhibition for the Glencore Xstrata Queensland Artists' Gallery, which is dedicated to profiling Queensland art and artists.

Another major component of our partnership with the Gallery is the Regional Queensland Touring Workshop Program, which takes art in its many forms to communities who wouldn't normally have the chance to experience it. The photography workshop offered by the Gallery in 2011 was particularly popular with the communities of Dalby, Wandoan, Miles, Bowen, Collinsville, Rolleston, Glenden, Springsure, Emerald and Mackay.

Glencore Xstrata congratulates the Gallery on its ongoing commitment to providing Queenslanders with opportunities to engage with art. We also acknowledge everyone who has contributed to the success of this longstanding partnership.

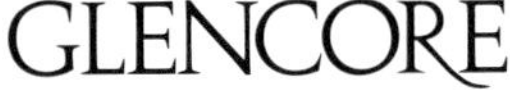

Breezeway, Yengarie Sugar Mill 1974, printed 2013

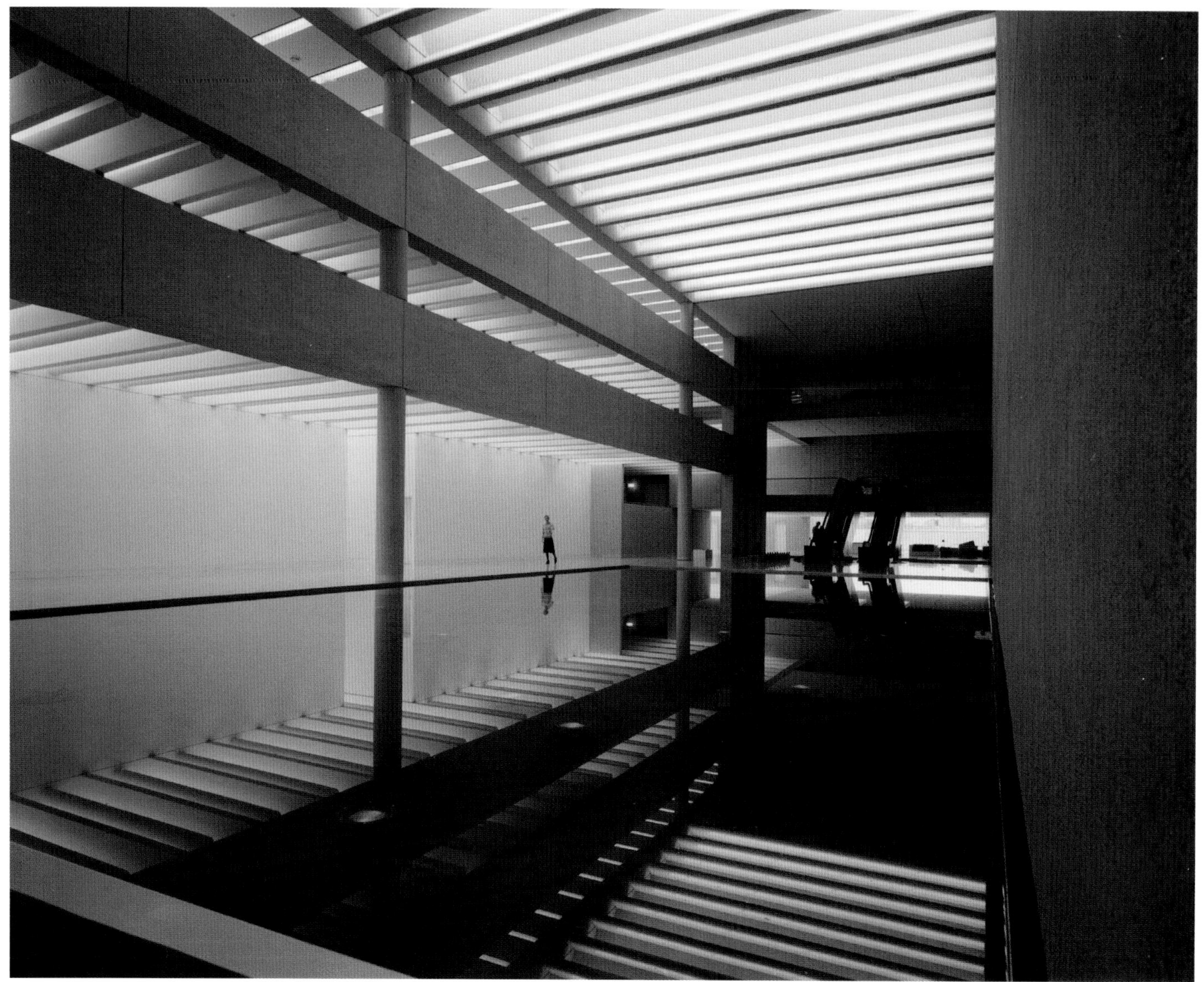

Queensland Art Gallery Watermall
1982, printed 2013

FOREWORD

Chris Saines CNZM
Director, Queensland Art Gallery | Gallery of Modern Art

The Queensland Art Gallery | Gallery of Modern Art is delighted to present this survey of the work of Richard Stringer, a renowned photographer, teacher and great friend of the Gallery. 'Pleasure of Place' spans over 40 years of eloquent image-making and includes many prints never before exhibited. These works offer us a focused lens through which to view the evolution of Queensland — from the decay of disused industrial landscapes to the ever burgeoning city and urban landscapes, and the people who reside within them.

Richard Stringer's beautiful and distinctive photographs often capture architecture, landscapes and industrial archaeology. Possibly thanks to his early training and practice as an architect, Stringer has an eye for intricate detail, a pronounced technical proficiency for composition and lighting, and a great sensitivity for the built environment that is immediately discernible. His approach to the human form is equally perceptive, illuminating the essence of his subjects and revealing strength of character.

Since the early 1970s, the Gallery has displayed a strong commitment to acquiring photographs that explore and document life in Queensland. Stringer, who continues in the tradition of other distinguished Australian documentary photographers, such as Harold Cazneaux and Max Dupain, is one of Queensland's most significant and singular contemporary proponents of this genre.

I congratulate Michael Hawker, Associate Curator, Australian Art, QAGOMA, curator of the exhibition, along with Richard Stringer himself and Sally Foster, Assistant Curator, International Art, for their contributions to this publication.

I particularly wish to thank Glencore Xstrata for continuing their visionary support of the Queensland Artists' Gallery. This partnership enables us to conduct research into the work of Queensland artists and promote their art, and this publication and exhibition demonstrate the enduring benefits this support has for art in this state.

Finally, and most importantly, I wish to very warmly thank Richard Stringer for preserving and illuminating Queensland life through his photographs. Richard and his wife Marguerite have worked extremely closely with us on 'Pleasure of Place' and it is thanks to them that we are able to present such a beautiful and evocative exhibition.

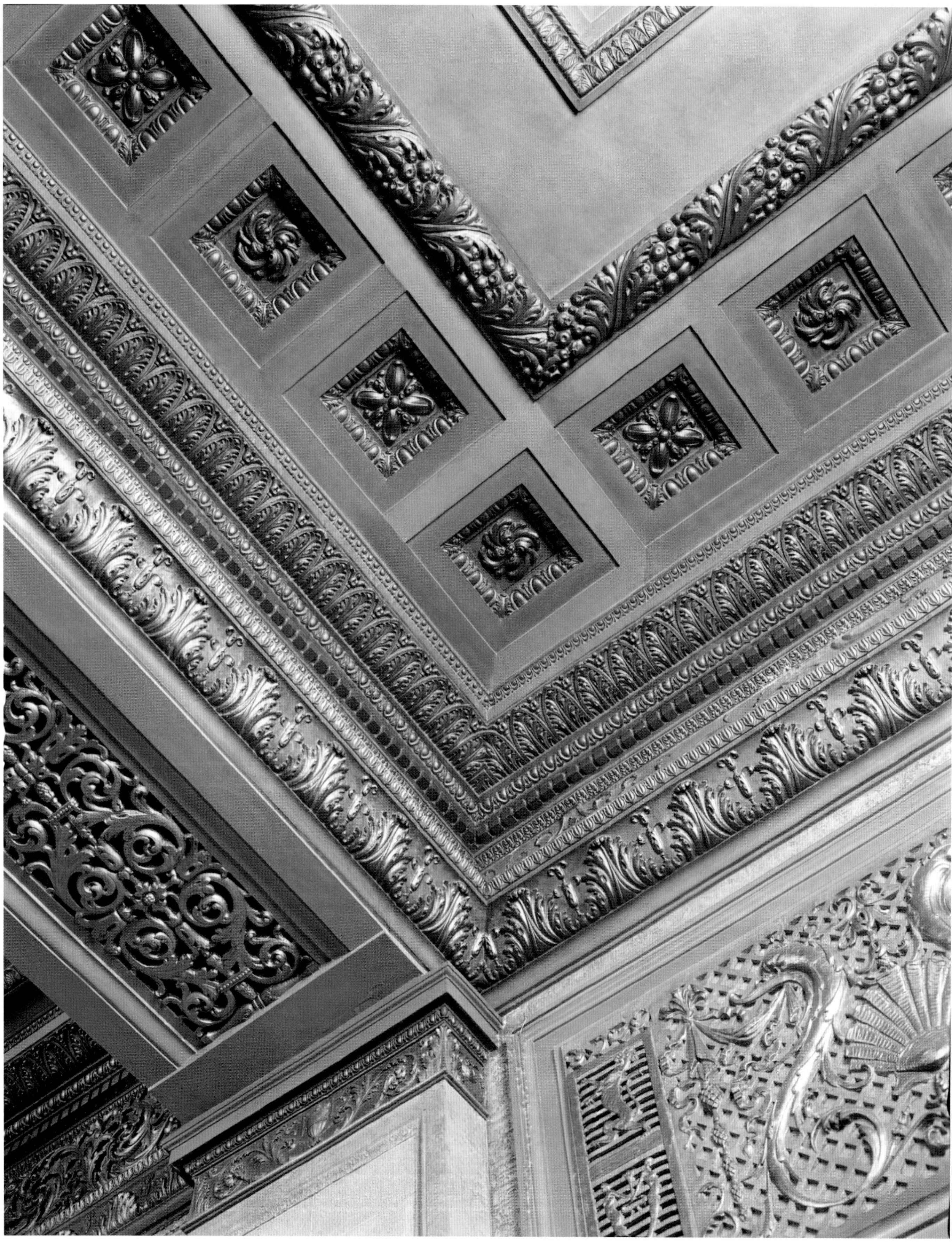

PLEASURE OF PLACE: PHOTOGRAPHS BY RICHARD STRINGER

Michael Hawker

> Every site has its own ethos. I like to research a site before I visit it. Once there, I like to walk through without the camera or sit and just observe. Eventually comes the realisation that unless I get moving, there will be no photographs, so the rest of the day is spent keeping up with the sun.[1]

Why is it that some photographs hold our interest and give us pleasure while others, apparently similar, do not? Despite photography's ubiquitous presence in our lives, we continue to struggle for an answer, all the while supported by the sureness and the intensity of our experience. Whether we delight in the form of the composition or our interest lies in the subject, there is no doubt that the most affecting photographs have a pictorial quality that commands our attention. The photographs of Richard Stringer are absorbing in exactly this way, and over his 40-year practice have demonstrated an enduring ability to engage the viewer.

Early developments in photography led to divergent aims: the desire to align the medium with the aesthetic traditions of nineteenth-century painting and the more pragmatic approach to use photography as a tool of factual documentation. Historically, photography has kept pace with the culture of scientific rationality and the desire to collect, assemble and order modern society in the museum and the archive. The start of the twentieth century saw the advent of photographic Modernism as marked by the rebuff of subjective Pictorialism and the turn to clear description and objectivity.[2] Even with the demise of pictorialist photography and the rise of 'factual' photography, the debate regarding form and content continued. The contest pitched the simple capacity of photography to produce a likeness against its ability to create a subtle artistic construct of 'fictive fact', revealing the essence of reality far more effectively than a straightforward replication.[3] If this personal response to the object is lacking, then the end result amounts to little more than a matter of pointing out what is there (under the guise of authenticity). Richard Stringer's images may therefore be considered in terms framed by curator Thomas Weski:

> If . . . the photographer succeeds in penetrating more deeply into the object, then we can relish in the photographer's observational ability to charge the familiar with additional meaning and we can enjoy the sensation of being confronted with a form of autonomy that we recognise from the world of visual art.[4]

THE MIND OF THE ARCHITECT

The overriding influence on Stringer's photography is his abiding attentiveness to architecture. Although Stringer was deeply influenced by his father photographing ballet dancers in postwar Melbourne, his attention turned to photography as a result of his training and practice in architecture.[5] While working as an architect in Brisbane in the 1960s, he realised how difficult it was for professional photographers to document architectural commissions. While architectural photography aims for accurate representation of a subject, it must, like all good photography, engage the viewer in a dialogue, one that conveys something of the art of the architect at the same time as it records the pragmatic concerns of design and structure. Stringer has spoken

Cornice, Regent Theatre, Brisbane 1975, printed 2013

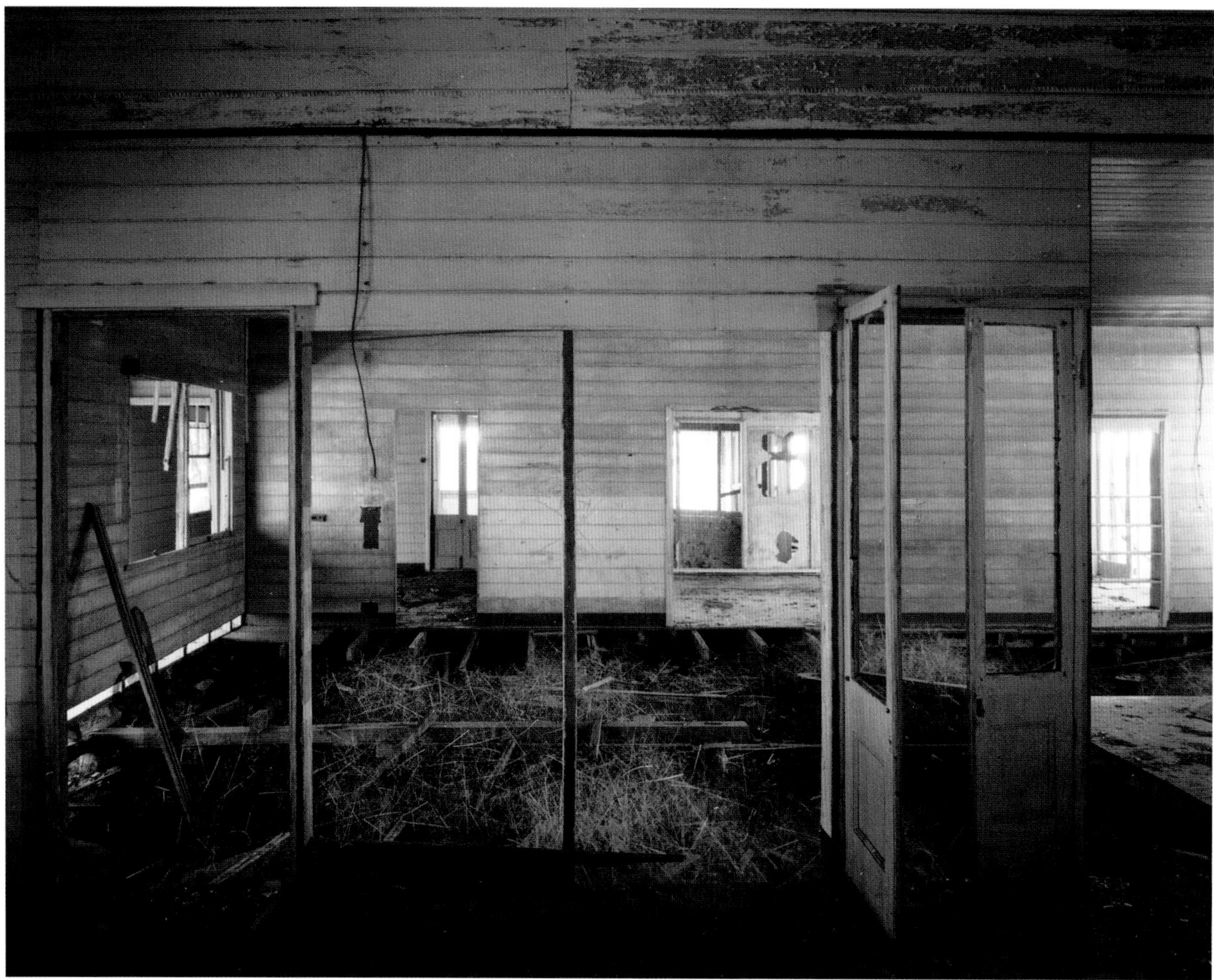

Manager's house, Ilfracombe Wool Scour 1975, printed 2013

Opposite: *Placing a sail unit, Sydney Opera House* 1967, printed 2013

of the challenge of the architectural photograph: 'The building has to be seen in relation to its surroundings. While a door knob might be significant, it is not the whole building'.[6]

Throughout the history of photography, architecture has proved a popular subject, mirroring our appreciation of both its cultural significance and its index of historical change. Stringer began documenting architecture when he established his own photographic business in 1967. He soon became Brisbane's architectural photographer of choice because of his nuanced understanding of the built environment and architectural principles. Stringer's practice expanded with commissions from the National Trust of Queensland and Sydney architect Howard Tanner to record historic buildings and gardens. As a result, his photography has played a major role in chronicling the architecture of Brisbane and Queensland, and his photographs have helped mark out the signature of many of the state's most successful architects of the past four decades.

Stringer is acutely aware of belonging to a continuing tradition of photography and is especially admiring of the Australian photographers Harold Cazneaux (1878–1953) and Max Dupain (1911–92). He is guided by the principles of documentary photography, addressing his subject with a keen eye honed by a desire to represent it as honestly as possible, while opening it to new interpretations and understandings. Like Cazneaux and Dupain, Stringer's compositions also convey the modernist mantra of structure, light and detail.

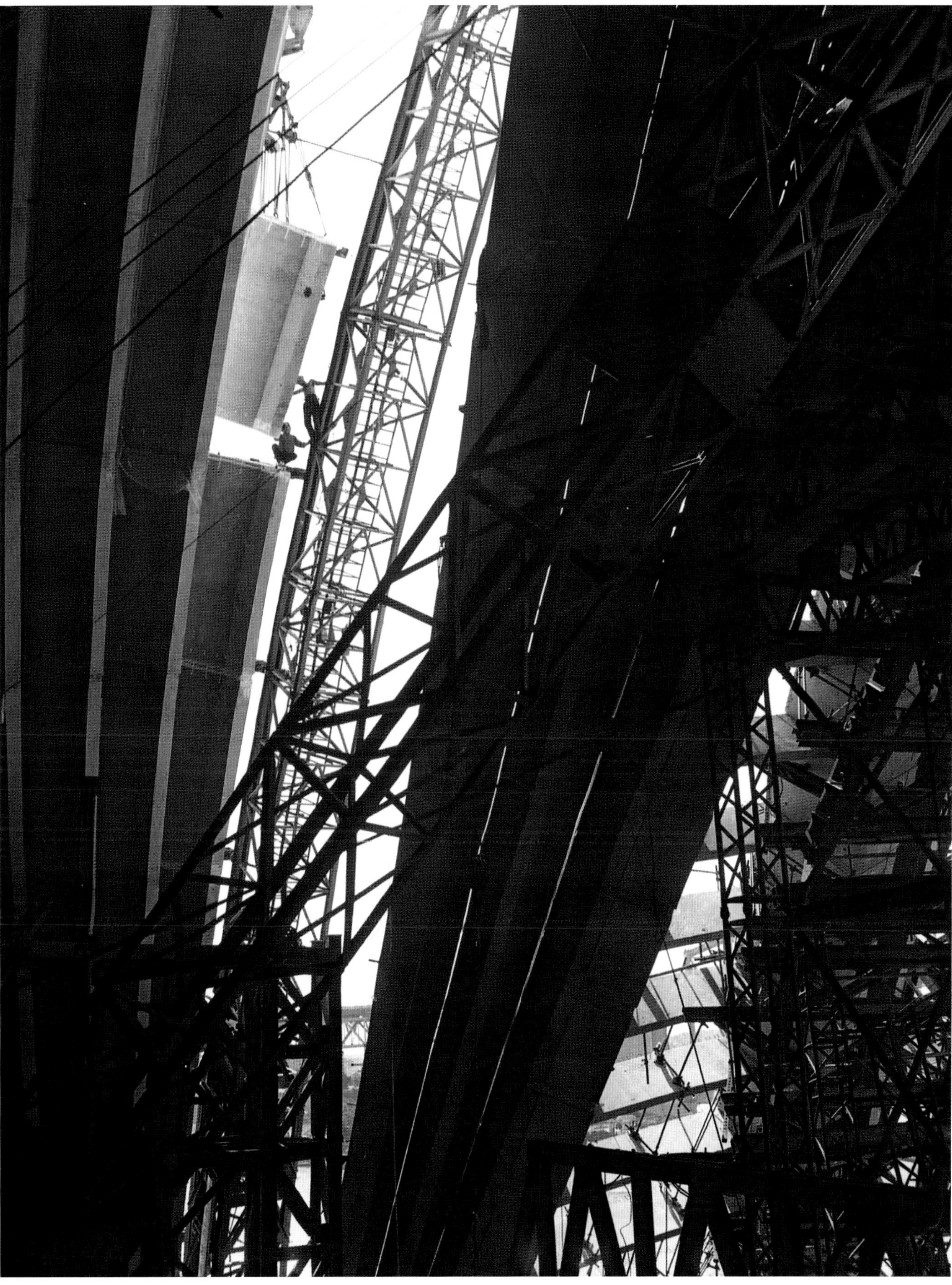

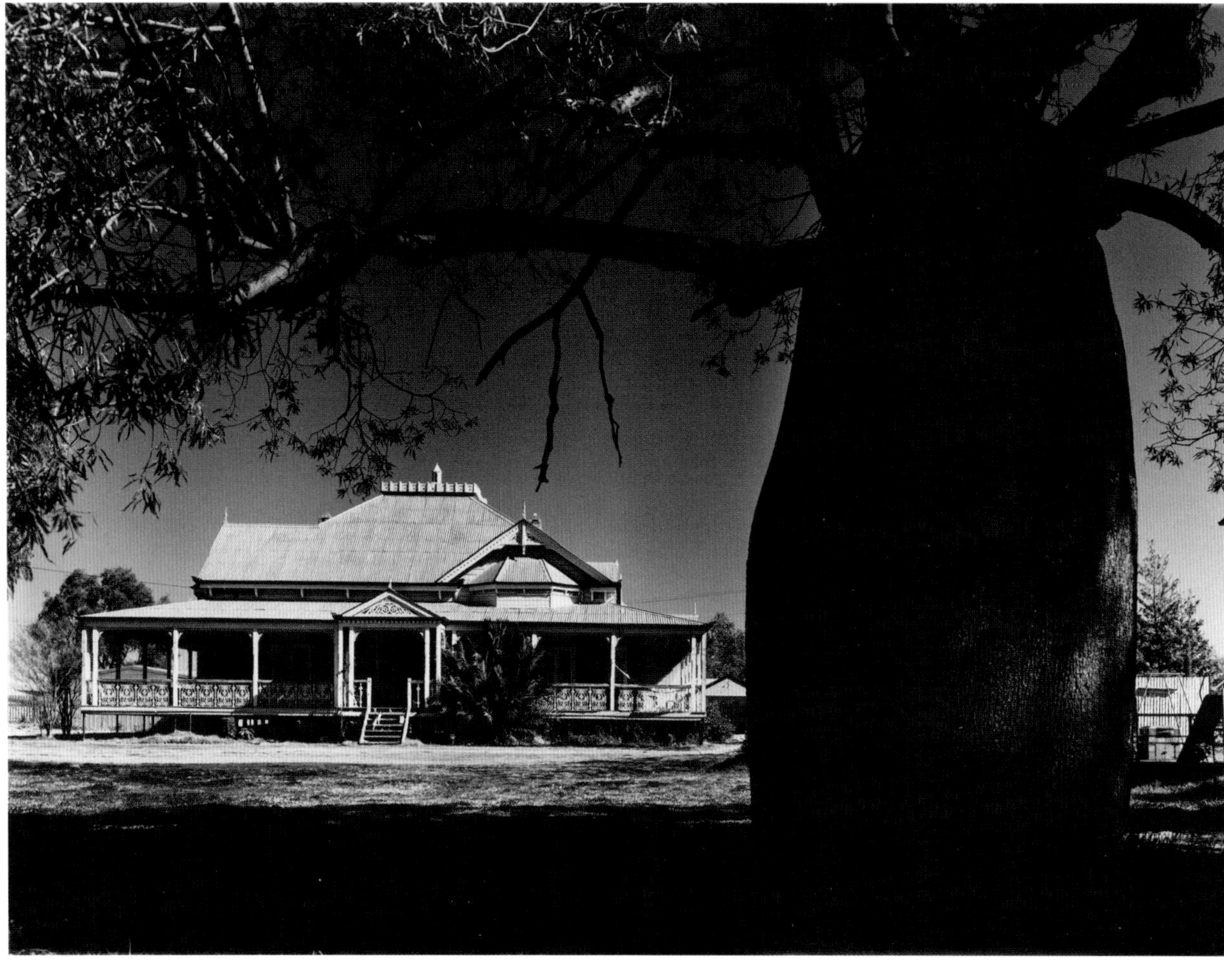

House, Roma 1982, printed 1987

Exterior architectural photography takes advantage of available daylight and the power and quality of light is of special importance to Stringer's compositions. Leaving very little to chance, he carefully calculates the position of the sun to determine the day's shooting schedule so as to achieve the best effects from his chosen locations. In architectural interiors, light falls differently, through doors, windows, skylights or from lighting fixtures, and under Stringer's control light articulates the character of place. A soft luminosity is achieved in *Manager's house, Ilfracombe Wool Scour* 1975,[7] for instance, where the derelict, floorless interior is lit by a row of windows to the rear of the building. Here, Stringer shows us an almost magical stillness in what was once a lively family home.

His compositions also communicate the aesthetic harmony of architecture and context. Taking advantage of foreground trees, statues or fountains, he leads the eye into the composition towards its central subject, the building. In *House, Roma* 1982, the elegance of a traditional Queenslander and the delicate lacework of its wrought iron veranda are framed by a bottle tree in the foreground. Deeply cast in shadow, the imposing tree trunk with its spreading branches just catches the light that falls full on the house behind. Elements are drawn together in simple and direct contrast — light, shade, lacework, tree trunk, timber and iron — and Stringer's governing principles of form and shadow, structure, light and detail are all at work.

PHOTOGRAPHER AS COLLECTOR

Once, when visiting the Stringers' home, my eye was caught by a framed photograph of the Bellevue Hotel. The Bellevue's overnight demolition in the late 1970s was under order from a state government with scant regard for Brisbane's cultural heritage.[8] What is remarkable about this image is that Stringer had added wooden fragments to the photograph, fragments of building materials taken directly from the demolition site. This instance of bricolage brings to mind a story about the esteemed American photographer Walker Evans (1903–75), who, near the end of his working life, was asked about the relationship between his habits as a collector and his work as a photographer: 'It's almost the same thing', he simply replied.[9]

Evans's prolific practice was characterised by photographs of everyday objects, road signs, discarded remnants and the like, all 'collected' through the act of photography. Collecting and photography share a faith in the 'taken object', as well as an understanding that this 'taking' is fundamentally transformative, implying that to make something, anything, the subject of a photograph is to appropriate it in some way and to insist it is worthy of attention, no matter how incidental or humble, or how essentially useful it may seem. Stringer is a bowerbird and chronicler, and these tendencies find their natural expression in the systematic recording of our environment, both built and natural.

A number of publications, particularly several produced by the Australian Council of National Trusts, demonstrate how Stringer's initial fascination with architecture attuned his eye to all manner of aspects of the historical environment.[10] He is one of the few photographers working in Queensland who has consistently sought out and recorded the design, craftsmanship and character of threatened buildings across the state. Over four decades, he has documented, collected and archived thousands of photographs to acknowledge what has been, what is and what may not be with us in the future. Stringer's architectural studies have helped him to understand what lies beneath the surface of things, they have taught him to look and to see, and to make things visible to those of us with untrained eyes, who look too quickly or too little.

PLEASURE OF RUINS

By 1963, Stringer had chosen to work with large-format cameras, giving him the ability to achieve a high level of detail in his images, as well as considerable control over perspective in order to emphasise order and structure. The view is always carefully selected to ensure its constituent elements combine to present a strong and engaging composition. This is particularly evident for what he calls his industrial archaeological subjects, where his aim is to:

> . . . see what has been made in the past . . . what it has become, and . . . to bring to the observer something of its past life and its present decay — decay which, in its slow return to the elements from which it came, has a beauty of its own.[11]

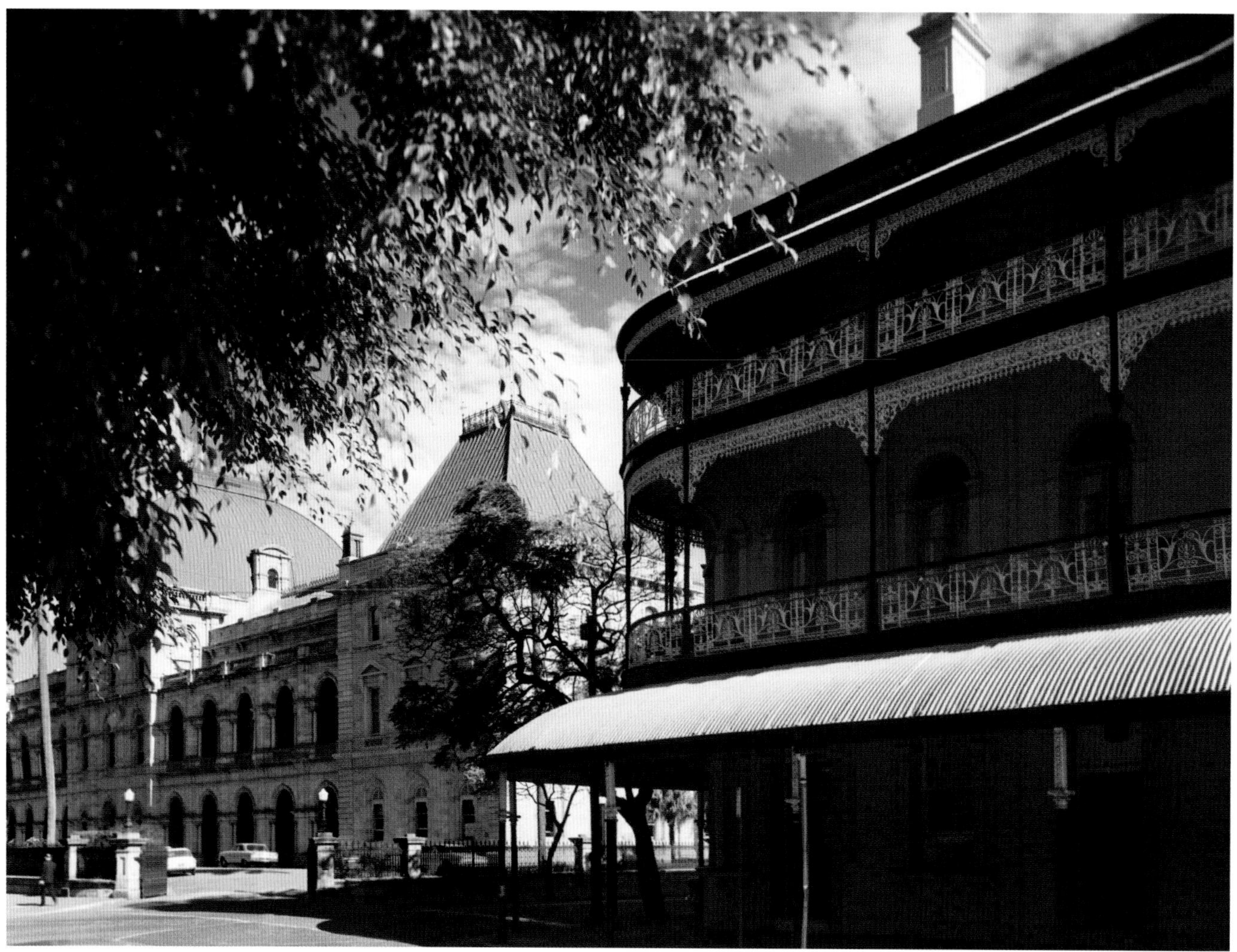

Curtain raiser, Bellevue precinct, Brisbane 1968, printed 2013

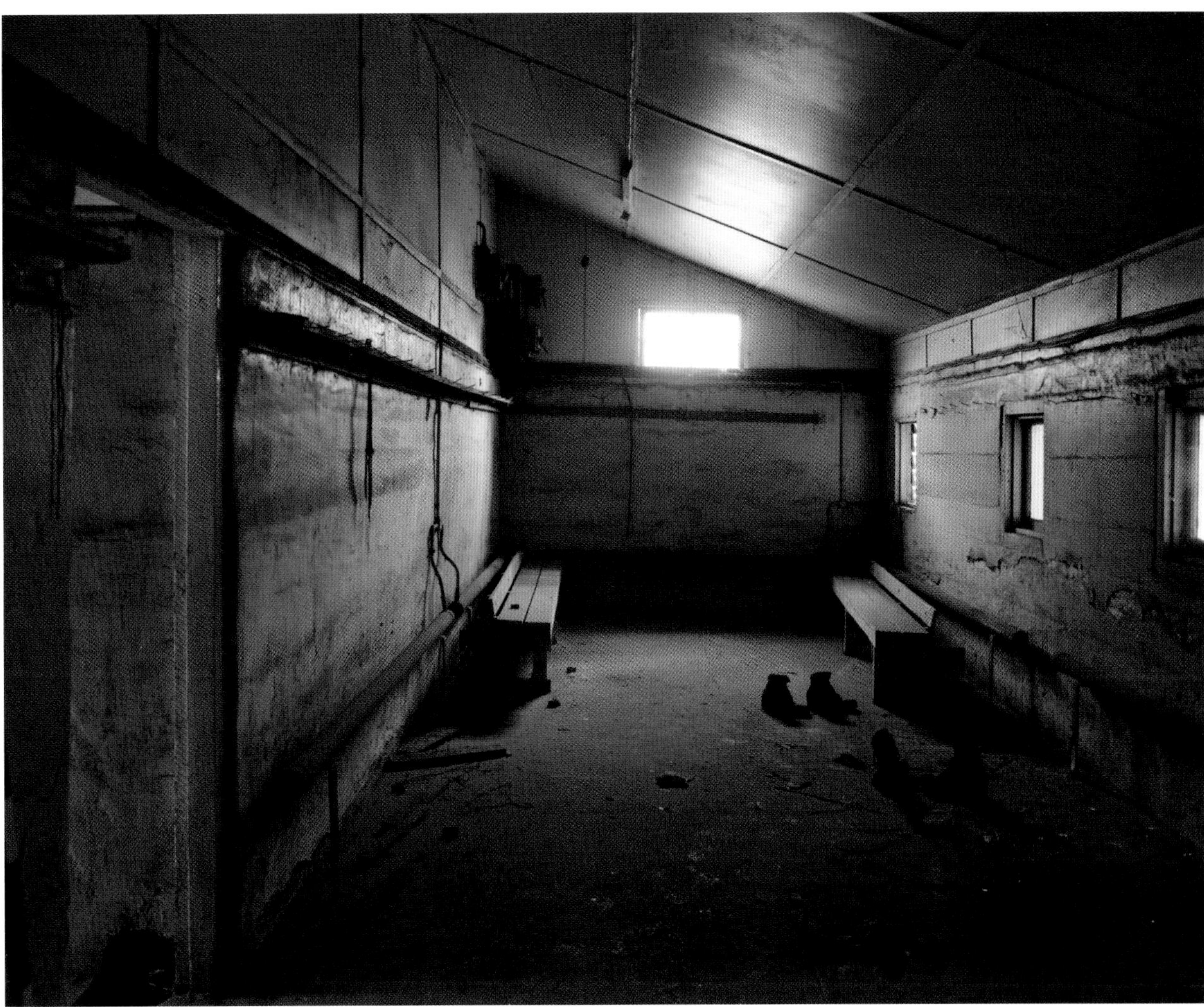

Door to the bath house, Rhondda Colliery 1990, printed 2013

His interest in ruins and dilapidated sites also points to the tradition described in *Pleasure of Ruins* (1953), in which Rose Macaulay writes of the contribution of ruins and their depiction to popular sensibility. As Macaulay argues, the Romanticism that swept European art and literature at the turn of the nineteenth century can be characterised by the fact that 'the human race is, and has always been, ruin-minded' and that 'all ages [have] found beauty in the dark and violent forces, physical and spiritual, of which ruin is one symbol'.[12] This sensibility is evident in many of Stringer's images, such as *Breezeway, Yengarie Sugar Mill* 1974, in which he records the sheer visual pleasure of the movement of grass buffeted by wind in the arched doorway of the ruined wall of an old mill — the symbol of nature taking back a landscape once emphatically inscribed with our making and dwelling. Similarly, *Goats, St Helena Prison* 1977 depicts two creatures standing sentinel-like on the collapsing prison walls, observing the photographer as he works. In capturing this unlikely moment, nature is seen as ultimately holding dominion over all.

In Stringer's work, there is always close consideration of the economic and historical influences on the environments he records. We see a scientific-like approach to stocktaking in his archive of these sites as an inquiry into the relationship between people and time. Stringer's photographs explore the social and cultural contexts that have led to current conditions, while the disquieting stillness of his images often belies the noisy history of the sites depicted: most of these works are black-and-white photographs, which lends them a timelessness associated with the documentary tradition. In *Door to the bath house, Rhondda Colliery* 1990, for example, a derelict interior is illuminated by window light, which draws the eye to wooden benches and pairs of discarded boots, symbols of the absent presence of boisterous miners and the working lives that shaped a community.

EDEN

Stringer's other enduring interest lies in responding to the natural world: whether a Stradbroke Island beachscape or the rich textures of grass and foliage in a bush setting, his works show a delight in the forms of nature. His photographs of nature are also based on the tenets of clarity and detail: we see the precise definition of grass stalks, ocean waves and rocky shores. The architect's eye remains alert to the structure and layering of vegetation in an organic architectural space.

Despite the rarity of colour in Stringer's works, he uses it to full effect to render the infinite chromatic range of vegetation and earth in its Eden-like state. We see this in *Pathway at Bumiera* 2010, which emphasises the constancy of nature, its twisted balletic structures filling a shimmering stage, and in the black-and-white *Gum trees, Mount Emu Creek* 1982, with its sculptural tree forms, or *Billabong Creek, Jerilderie* 1986, with its foreground tonal variations of grasses and flowers. Although Stringer notes that he initially 'chose to ignore colour in preference for black and white . . . because the photographs lasted better and I could do everything myself', with advances in digital reproduction earlier problems have been eliminated allowing him to 'enjoy the level of control now possible in dealing digitally with tone and colour'.[13] A beautiful use of colour is also evident in *Slag blockwork, Mt Chalmers Copper and Gold Mine* 1975, where he captures the colours of variegated copper in the blockwork created from mining slag, which, in turn, has been weathered by time.

A PORTRAIT OF THE ARTIST

Although the human figure rarely intrudes into the frame of Stringer's photographs, their spectral forms inhabit many works. Like the work of French photographer Eugène Atget (1857–1927), who documented Paris, Stringer's photographs of the built environment are redolent of a human presence. Stringer is in fact a fine portrait photographer: his proficiency in conveying something very specific of his sitters' individuality is always apparent. *Luke Roberts, Bellas Gallery* 1988 addresses the artist's theatrical persona while maintaining the sense of performance as farce, while in *Anne Wallace* 2004, Stringer frames the artist in what appears to be one of her own oil paintings. The architect's eye combines the geometric formalism of the interior of the artist's home with the confident stance of Wallace in a doorway. Stringer's portraits all share an engagement with the subject, an understanding and an appreciation of a kindred spirit, and these artist portraits play a significant role in recording the cultural life of a city through its people.

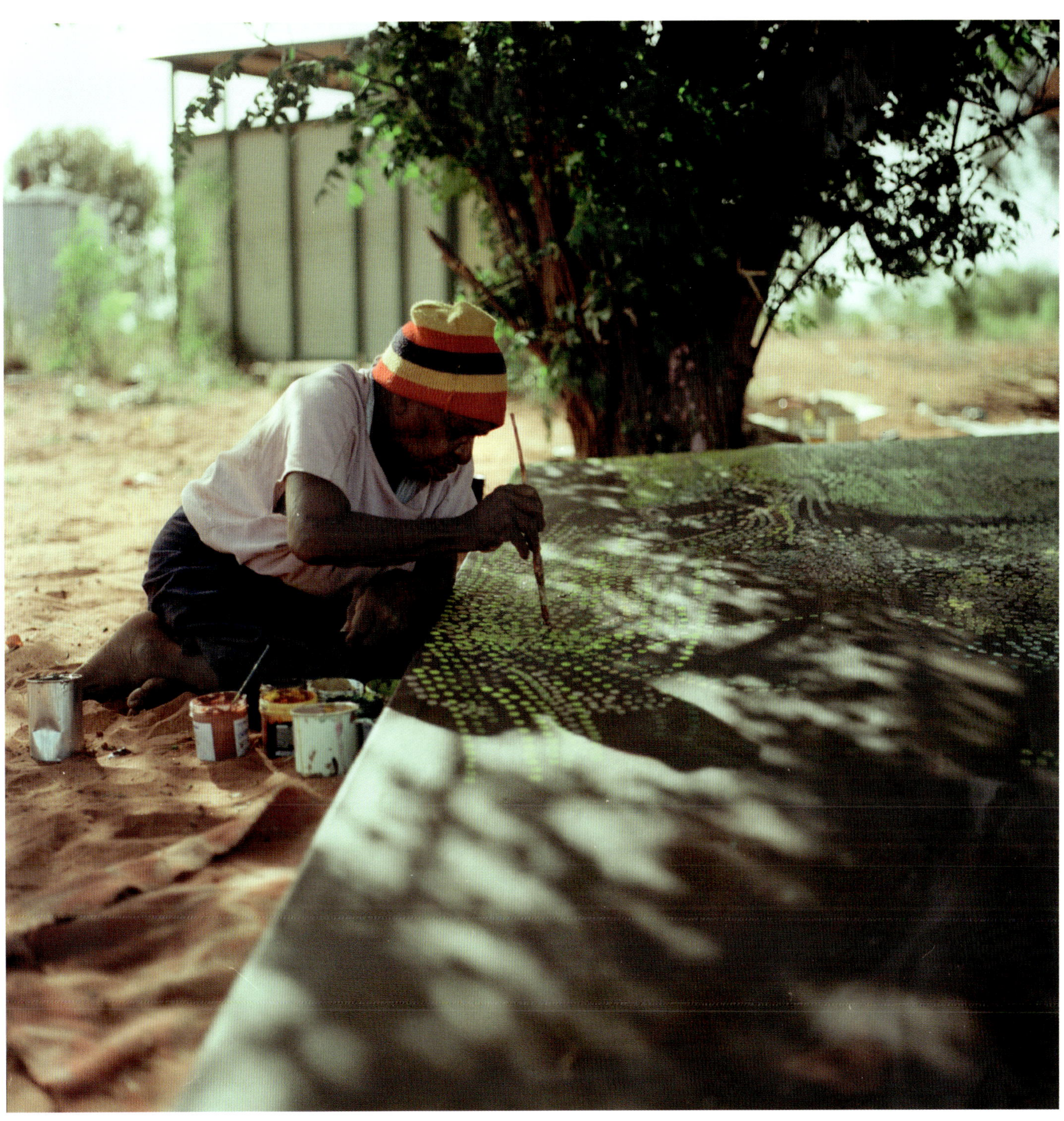

Emily Kame Kngwarreye in her studio 1991, printed 2013

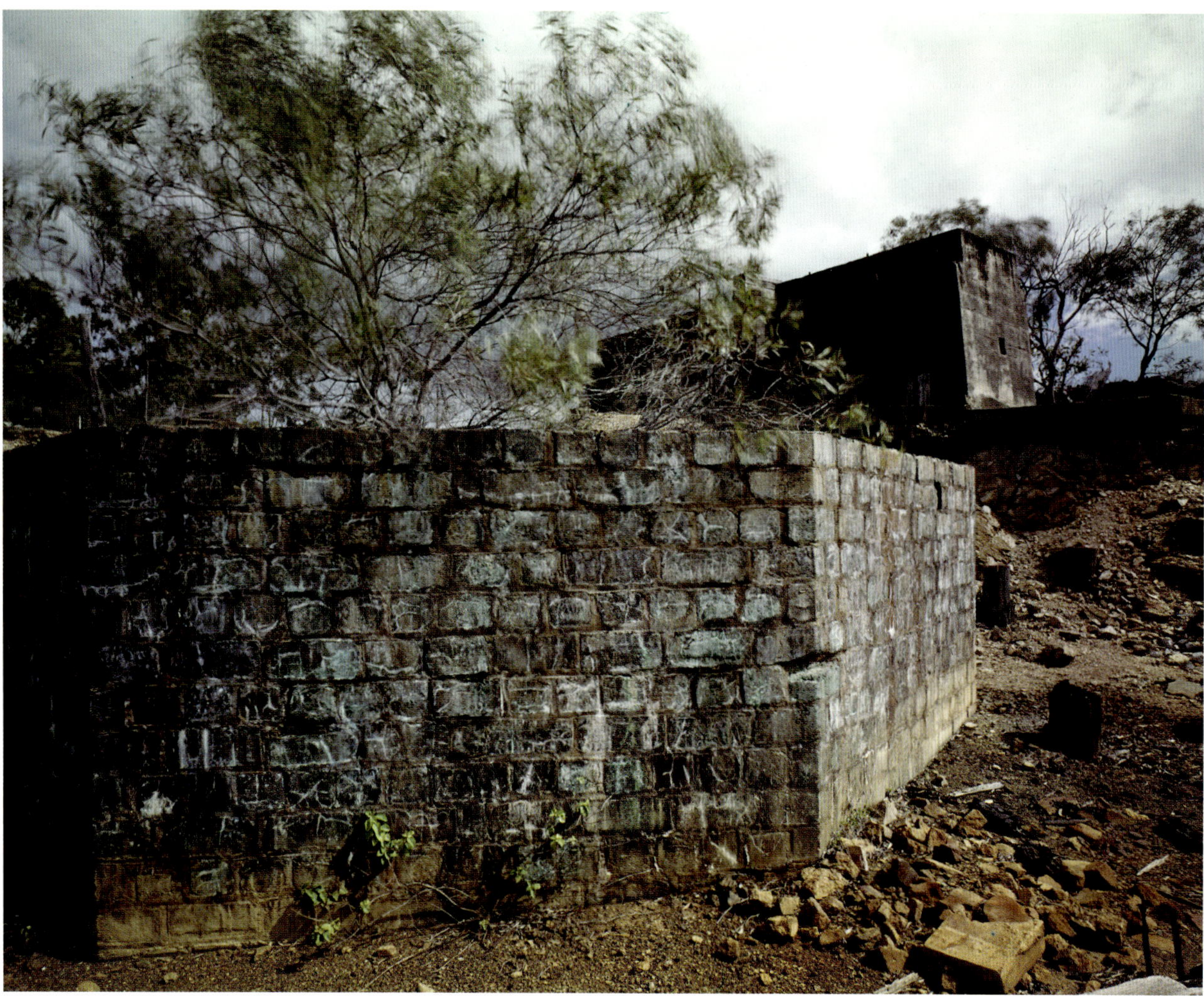

Slag blockwork, Mt Chalmers Copper and Gold Mine 1975, printed 2013

The images featured in *Pleasure of Place: Photographs by Richard Stringer* span the creative work of a lifetime; at the same time, they merely glance at the surface of Stringer's prodigious output. They reveal the remarkable achievements of an artist who has diligently pursued his craft, while always considering the ineffable sense of what makes a great image, and how photography can amplify the qualities of what appears before the lens. At the centre of Stringer's unique achievement lies a sense of history; the continuum permeates his work and brings the past to us in the present so it may be preserved for future audiences. According to the artist:

> I decided that maybe I could make people aware of this by making them look . . . I could exploit the veracity of photographs if I showed things in the way that they were experienced and without any trickery.[14]

Here, we see something of the photographer himself, and what continues to drive and inform his passion for the medium. There is much to admire and celebrate in the photography of Richard Stringer.

Michael Hawker is Associate Curator, Australian Art, Queensland Art Gallery | Gallery of Modern Art.

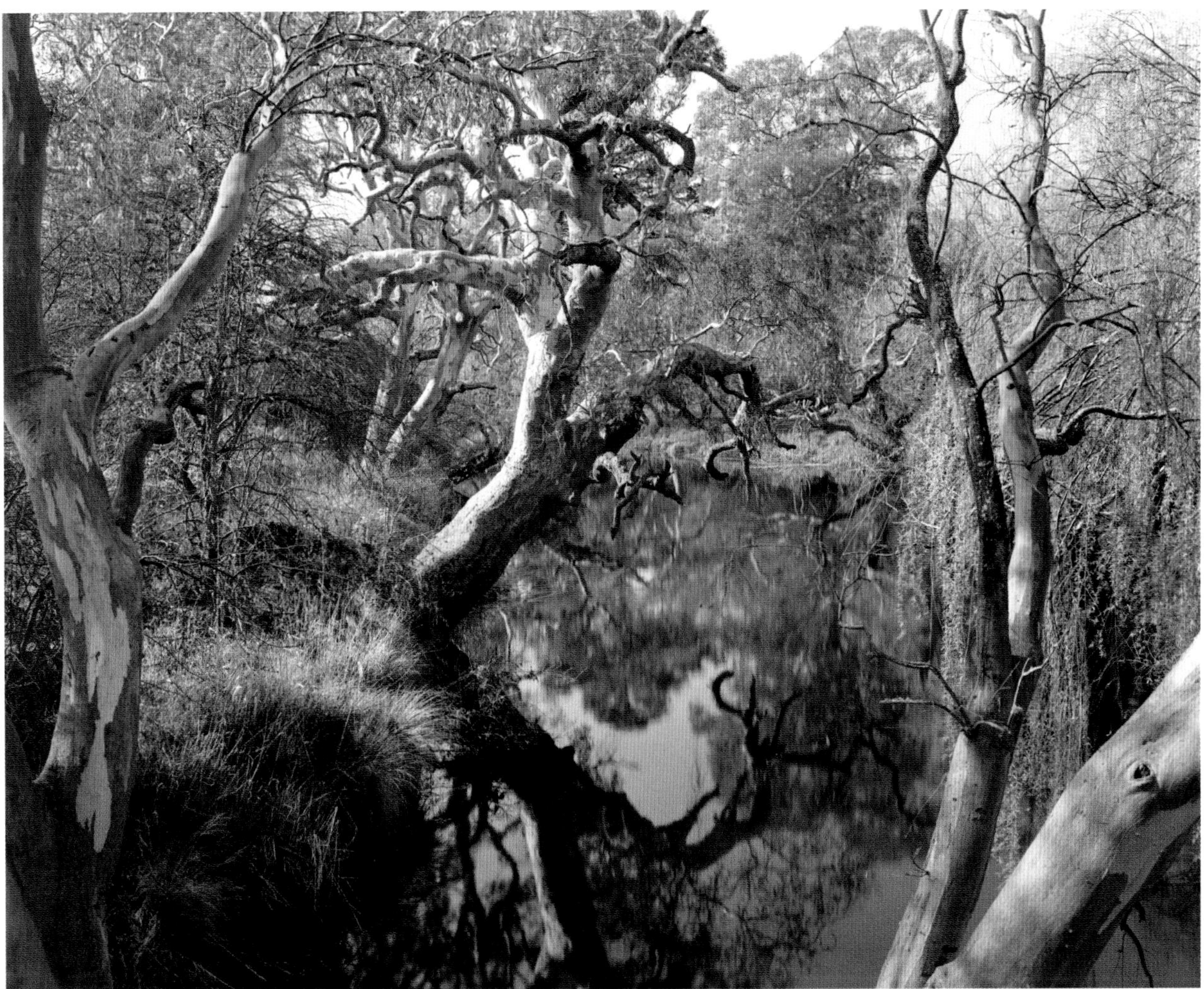

Gum trees, Mount Emu Creek 1982, printed 2013

Endnotes

1 Richard Stringer, *Industrial Archaeology: Photographs of Ipswich's Industrial Heritage* [exhibition catalogue], Ipswich Regional Art Gallery, Ipswich, 1993, unpaginated.

2 See David Campany, '"Almost the same thing": Some thoughts on the collector-photographer', in Emma Dexter and Thomas Weski (eds.), *Cruel and Tender: The Real in the Twentieth-Century Photograph* [exhibition catalogue], Tate, London, 2003, p.33.

3 Thomas Weski, 'Cruel and tender', in Dexter and Weski, p.23.

4 Weski, p.23.

5 Stringer's father was a keen amateur photographer who documented over five decades of Australian dance, including the work of resident companies and visiting troupes.

6 Richard Stringer, interview with Michael Hawker, Brisbane, 6 September 2013.

7 This is the house where the Governor-General, Her Excellency the Honourable Quentin Bryce, AC, CVO, spent some of her childhood, as her father was the manager of the Ilfracombe Wool Scour.

8 The once prestigious Bellevue Hotel (built 1885–86) was located on the corner of George and Alice Streets in Brisbane's CBD. In 1973, the Queensland government had plans to demolish the Bellevue and redevelop the block by constructing office buildings, but pressure from the National Trust and members of the public resulted in a temporary reprieve. Early the morning of 20 April 1979, the government sent the Deen Brothers demolition firm, accompanied by police, to demolish the Bellevue; over 700 people turned up to protest the destruction.

9 Campany, p.33.

10 For a selected list of publications, see 'Biography', in *Pleasure of Place: Photographs by Richard Stringer* [exhibition catalogue], Queensland Art Gallery, Brisbane, 2013, p.37.

11 Stringer, *Industrial Archaeology: Photographs of Ipswich's Industrial Heritage*, unpaginated.

12 Rose Macaulay, *Pleasure of Ruins*, William Clowes and Sons, London, 1953, p.20.

13 See Richard Stringer, 'Technical commentary', in *Pleasure of Place: Photographs by Richard Stringer*, p.34.

14 Stringer, 'Technical commentary', p.34.

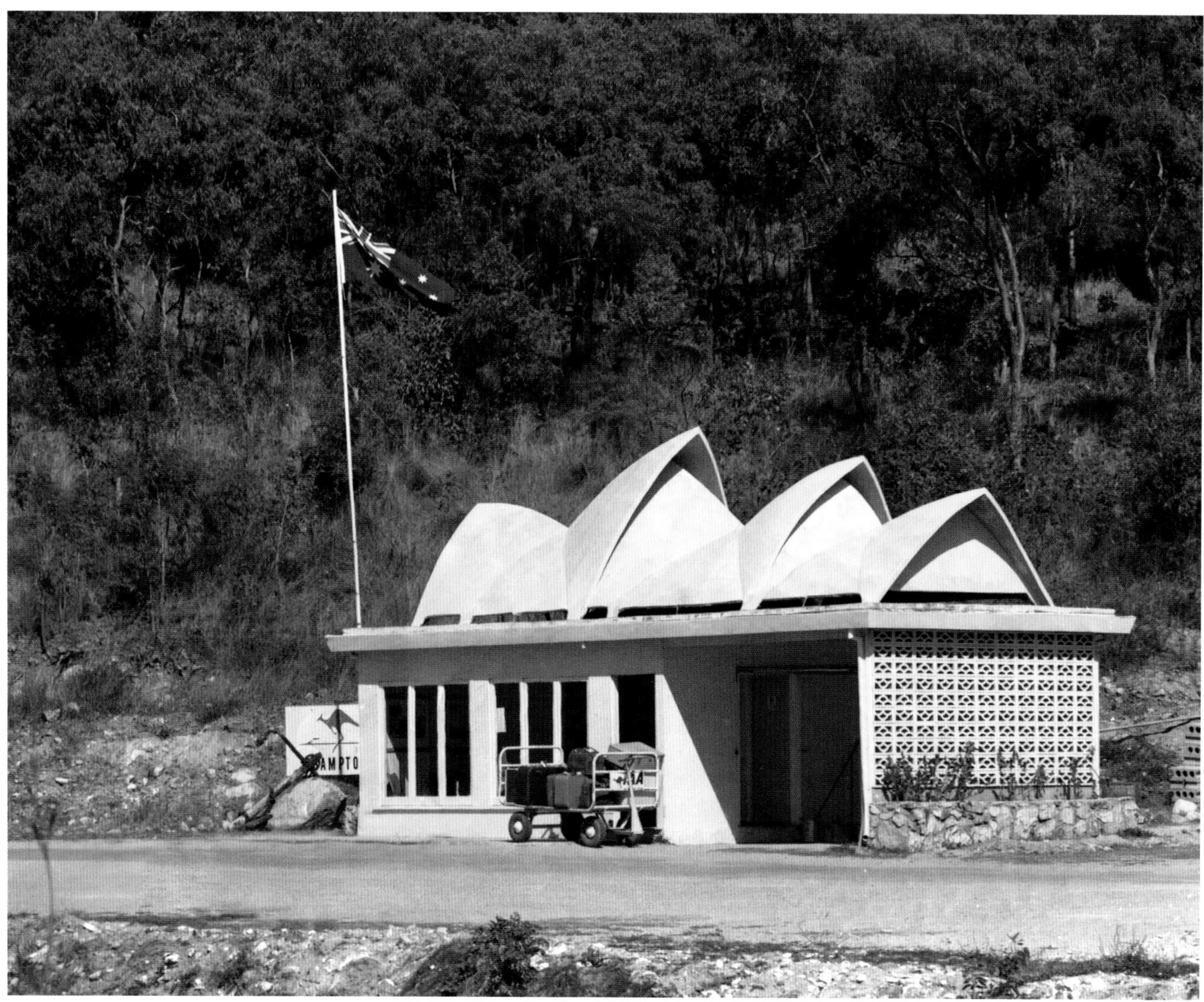

Brampton Island Airport 1968,
printed 2013

BEFORE THE SERVICE STATION: THE EARLY PHOTOGRAPHS

Sally Foster

When I first saw Richard Stringer's photograph *Brampton Island Airport* 1968, showing a modest concrete brick building with a replica of the Sydney Opera House shells sitting atop its roof, it immediately brought to mind the phrase 'the decorated shed', coined by the authors of the 1972 Yale University study *Learning From Las Vegas*.[1] The term was used to describe a simple structure that has been embellished with an applied symbol, in opposition to early and mid-century modern architecture where integrity and originality in design called for structures to stand alone, with all unnecessary adornment omitted. In the case of Brampton Island's airport, the applied symbol of the Sydney Opera House made, if not an original statement, then a radically contemporary one when Stringer took this photograph in 1968 and it was published in the modern architecture newsletter *Cross-Section*.[2] The shells of the Jørn Utzon-designed building were only completed in 1967, and the Opera House itself was not finished and opened until 1973.

Taken five years before the publication of *Learning From Las Vegas*, this photograph by Stringer was clearly not influenced by its analysis of the commercial roadside architecture of the famous American casino strip. What the photograph does suggest, however, along with a number of other notable examples from the period — such as Bernard Rudofsky's 1964–65 exhibition 'Architecture without Architects: A Short Introduction to Non-Pedigreed Architecture', and accompanying publication, at the Museum of Modern Art, New York[3] — is that the serious study of what was broadly termed vernacular architecture had become a subject of international importance in the mid 1960s. A number of architects, academics and cultural theorists sought to reinvigorate the debates surrounding the more 'puristic' aspects of orthodox mid-century modern architecture by looking with renewed interest at examples of the ordinary and the vernacular.

Before becoming a professional architectural photographer around 1967, Richard Stringer trained and briefly practiced as an architect. He graduated with a Bachelor of Architecture from the University of Melbourne in 1960, having studied during the late 1950s, when European and American Modernism were at the height of their critical and academic influence, and when, conversely, the particularities of Australia's cultural climate became increasingly important for local design. What becomes clear from conversations with Stringer is how important this time was for his creative development. Fundamental to an appreciation of the refined simplicity in his highly detailed photographs is an understanding that there is no incongruity between his formal training as an architect and the photographic archive of vernacular, and often derelict, Queensland buildings amassed over the course of his 40-year career.

During the late 1950s, the University of Melbourne employed a number of highly regarded Australian- and European-trained teachers in the Fine Arts Department and School of Architecture, who exerted an enormous influence on Richard Stringer's approach to seeing and analysing the world. Two innovative and inspiring teachers stand out as having a profound and lasting effect: Austrian-trained architect Fritz Janeba (1905–83) and architectural historian David Saunders (1928–86). Fritz Janeba, who had trained at the Akademie der bildenden Künste in Vienna, taught at the

School of Architecture at the University of Melbourne from 1946 (the year the department was established) until 1960. Janeba's intellectual background and schooling in the iconoclastic design of Walter Gropius (1883–1969) and (Ludwig) Mies van der Rohe (1886–1969) informed his philosophical approach to teaching the rational principles of European Modernism — essentially, economy of design for maximum effect. However, he equally instructed his students to engage in a dialogue with the specific conditions of everyday life — form follows function.[4] By emphasising the importance of developing the skills to think about and look objectively at physical objects, whether a telephone or a building, in order to fully grasp the detail of their design and construction, Janeba taught Stringer to look and to see.

David Saunders lectured in architectural history at the University of Melbourne from 1956 until 1968, and over the course of his academic career undertook important research for organisations such as the National Trust of Australia and the Australian Heritage Commission. Introducing the study of Australian architecture to the university syllabus, Saunders would send his students to look at buildings around the city, encouraging them to approach the evaluation of historic buildings with the same analytical objectivity as they would examples of modern architecture.[5] Melbourne was not only endowed with a thriving postwar architectural scene, the city also retained many important examples of nineteenth-century provincial architectural styles, as well as early modern designs by architects such as Harold Desbrowe-Annear (1865–1933), who was at the forefront of Melbourne's Arts and Craft Movement in the 1890s, together with the Prairie School-influenced buildings of Walter Burley Griffin (1876–1937) and Marion Griffin (1871–1961). Saunders taught Stringer that architecture had a timeline — incorporating both construction and decay — into which fell a variety of styles and forms that warranted close attention and, importantly, not all of which had been designed by architects.

When Richard Stringer moved to Brisbane in 1963 he worked briefly for James Birrell (b.1928). Birrell, also a University of Melbourne graduate, had moved to Brisbane in 1955 and become the architect for Brisbane City Council, where he played a significant role in reshaping the city's postwar civic landscape.[6] It was around this time that Stringer became aware of the need for professional photographers who could translate the express wishes of the modern architect and document particular aspects of finished buildings, paying particular attention to specific design elements. As a consequence, Stringer, who had never intended to become a photographer, set up a small photographic business designed to cater to this niche market.

Almost from the beginning, Stringer began using a 5x4 large-format camera. Tripod-mounted and time-intensive, large-format cameras were more commonly associated with nineteenth-century landscape photography and studio portraiture and allowed for greater control over perspective, while producing large negatives with an extraordinary level of detail. In addition to his professional commissions, Stringer began photographing buildings he found interesting from an architectural viewpoint. As art historian Ihor Holubizky has pointed out, however, Stringer did not conform to the

Church at Gatton 1967, printed 2013

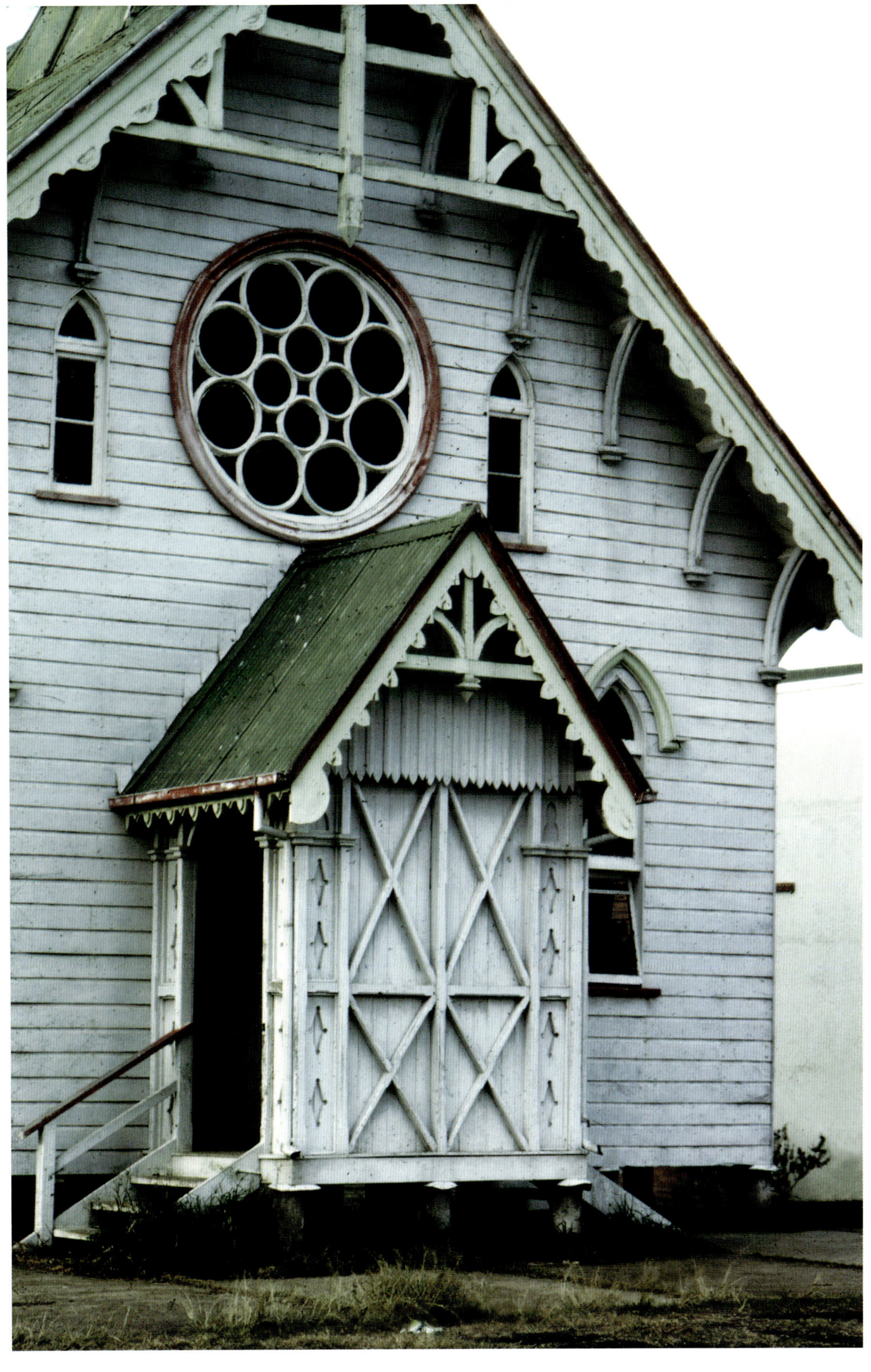

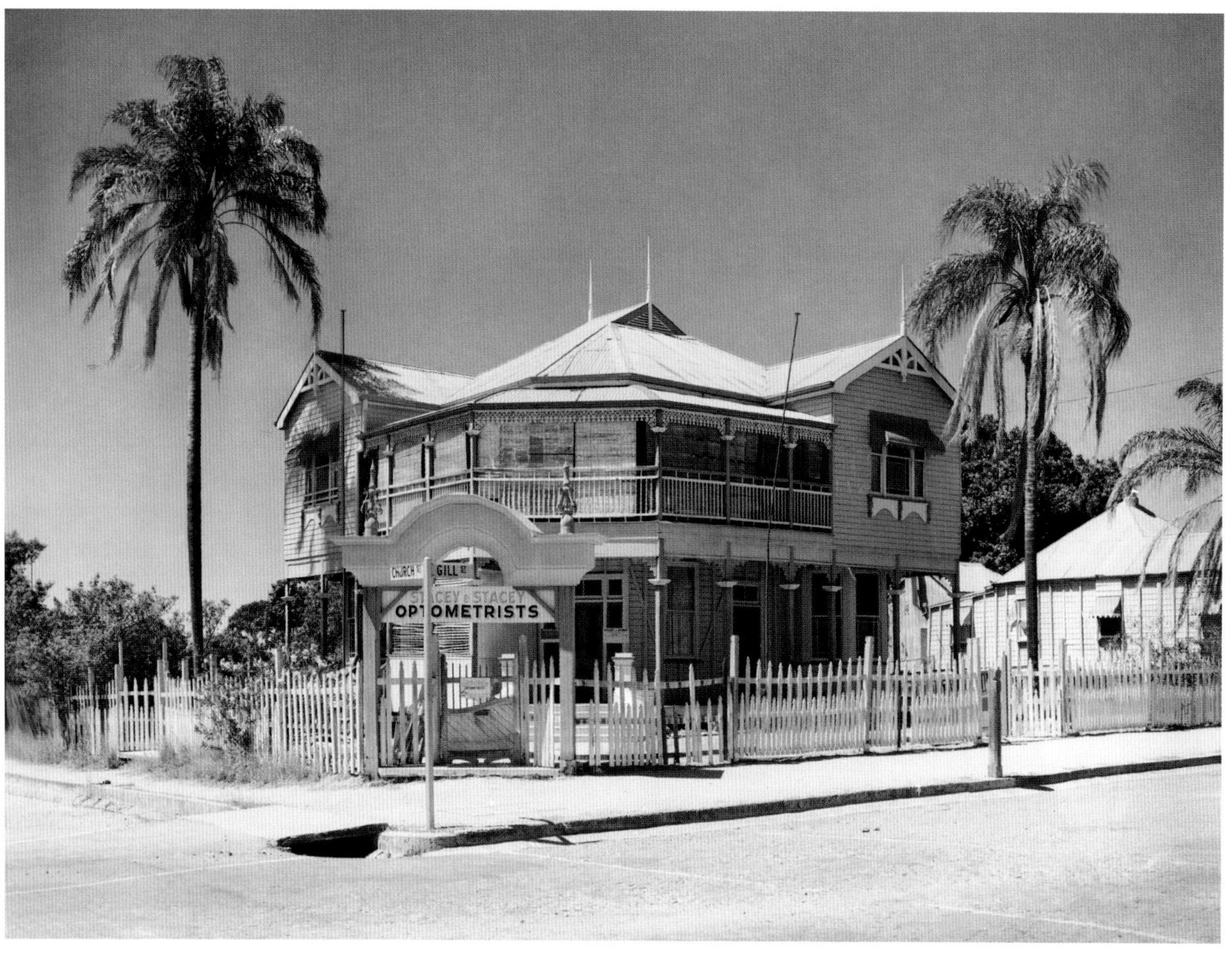

Before the service station, Charters Towers 1966, printed 2013

genre of architectural photography as it was practiced in the mid twentieth century by American photographer Julius Shulman (1910–2009), amongst others.[7] Shulman's images of modern Californian architecture, such as the Richard Neutra-designed *Kaufmann House, Palm Springs* 1946 and Pierre Koenig's *Case Study House #22, Los Angeles* 1960 — designed to show off the merits of modern design to the broader architectural community, as well as to the expanding commercial sector — became iconic representations of American Modernism in their own right. It is by comparison with a photographer like Shulman that we can perhaps most clearly see just how influential figures like Janeba and Saunders were for Stringer's philosophical approach to architectural photography.

With equivalent objectivity, Stringer photographed modern architecture alongside ordinary or industrial or once majestic buildings in various states of collapse. A run-down Queenslander being used as an optometrist's office in *Before the service station, Charters Towers* 1966, the beautiful geometric architectural detail in *Church at Gatton* 1967, a concrete replica of a classical Greek statue at the entrance of Brisbane's Rydges Motel in *Morning on St Paul's Terrace* 1970, or indeed the 'Sydney Opera House' on the roof of a shed on Brampton Island — all receive equal attention as photographic subjects.[8] As a consequence, Stringer has created a photographic archive owing more artistically and aesthetically to the simple but exacting images of vernacular American architecture from the 1930s by Walker Evans (1903–75), than to the highly polished images of Julius Shulman.

It is difficult for me to look at Stringer's photographs and not draw comparisons with those of Walker Evans. In large part, this is due to the buildings Evans photographed throughout America — often wooden and in varying states of ruin — and the type of vernacular architecture found in Queensland. However, it is also because of the manner in which the photographers approached their respective subject matter. Seeking the 'real' America, Evans traversed the country, photographing ordinary people and architecture in a seemingly 'straight' manner, free from pictorial artifice and stylistic mannerisms. Nonetheless, Evans was painstakingly aware of the way his subjects were framed and transformed into images. Writing in 1938, arts patron Lincoln Kirstein wrote of Evans's architectural photographs:

> His eye is on symbolic fragments of nineteenth century American taste, crumpled pressed-tin Corinthian capitals, debased baroque ornament, wooden rustication and cracked cast-iron moulding, survivals of our early imperialistic expansion . . . Evans has employed a knowing and hence respectful attitude to explore the consecutive tradition of our primitive monuments, an advanced philosophy and ideological technique to record their simplicity.[9]

With his eye on the architectural fragments of nineteenth- and twentieth-century parochial Australian tastes, and his respectful attitude to our historical buildings, Richard Stringer compiled from the 1960s onwards an unparalleled photographic archive of Queensland's lost architecture.

Sally Foster is Assistant Curator, International Art, Queensland Art Gallery | Gallery of Modern Art.

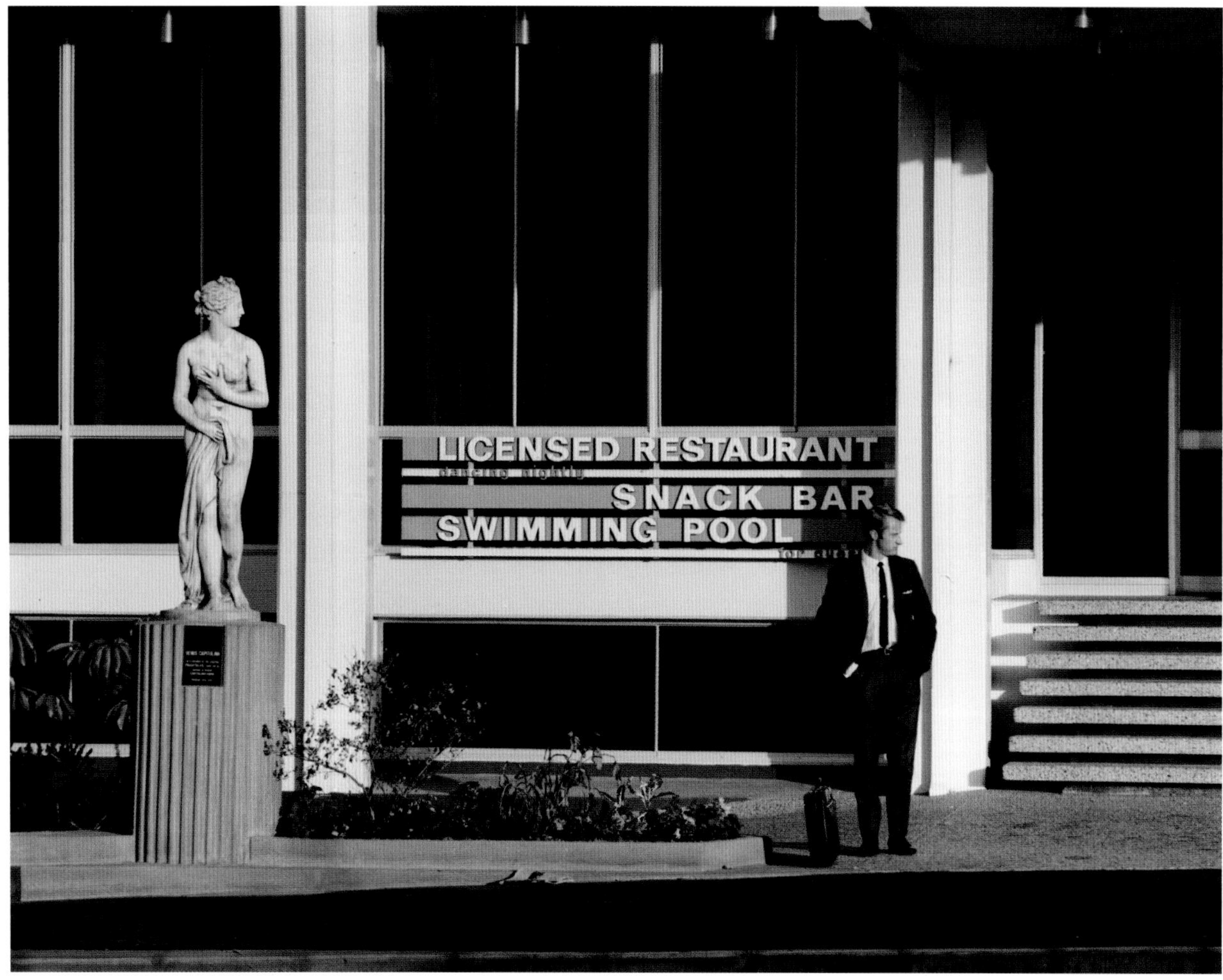

Morning on St Paul's Terrace 1970, printed 2013

Opposite: *Independent Church, Melbourne* 1977, printed 2013

Endnotes

1 Robert Venturi, Denise Scott Brown and Steven Izenour, *Learning From Las Vegas: The Forgotten Symbolism of Architectural Form* [revised edition], The MIT Press, Cambridge, Massachusetts, 1977, p.87.

2 The journal *Cross-Section* was founded by architect Robin Boyd in 1952 and published by the School of Architecture, University of Melbourne, until 1971. The journal is available online through the University of Melbourne Library.

3 Bernard Rudofsky, *Architecture without Architects: A Short Introduction to Non-Pedigreed Architecture* [second edition], Museum of Modern Art, New York, 1965.

4 For a discussion of the life and work of Fritz Janeba, see Anne Brennan, 'A philosophical approach to design: Gerhard Herbst and Fritz Janeba', in Roger Butler (ed.), *The Europeans: Emigré Artists in Australia, 1930–1960* [exhibition catalogue], National Gallery of Australia, Canberra, 1997, pp.153–66.

5 For David Saunders's biographical details, see Judith Brine, 'Saunders, David Arthur Lewis (1928–1986)', *Australian Dictionary of Biography*, http://adb.anu.edu.au/biography/saunders-david-arthur-lewis-15756, viewed 11 July 2013.

6 For a discussion of James Birrell's architecture, see Andrew Wilson, 'California dreaming: Civic ambition and subtropical housing in postwar Queensland', in Miranda Wallace and Sarah Stutchbury (eds.), *Place Makers: Contemporary Queensland Architecture* [exhibition catalogue], Queensland Art Gallery, Brisbane, 2008, p.31.

7 See Ihor Holubizky, 'Peter Liddy + Richard Stringer: The industrial cycle (more than washing the past)', in Peter Liddy and Richard Stringer (eds.), *Industrial Cycle: Photographs of the North Ipswich Railway Workshops*, CDE Communications, Annerley, Qld, 2003, p.11.

8 All the buildings depicted in these photographs have since been demolished.

9 Lincoln Kirstein, 'Photographs of America: Walker Evans', in *Walker Evans: American Photographs* [75th anniversary edition], Museum of Modern Art, New York, 2012, p.197.

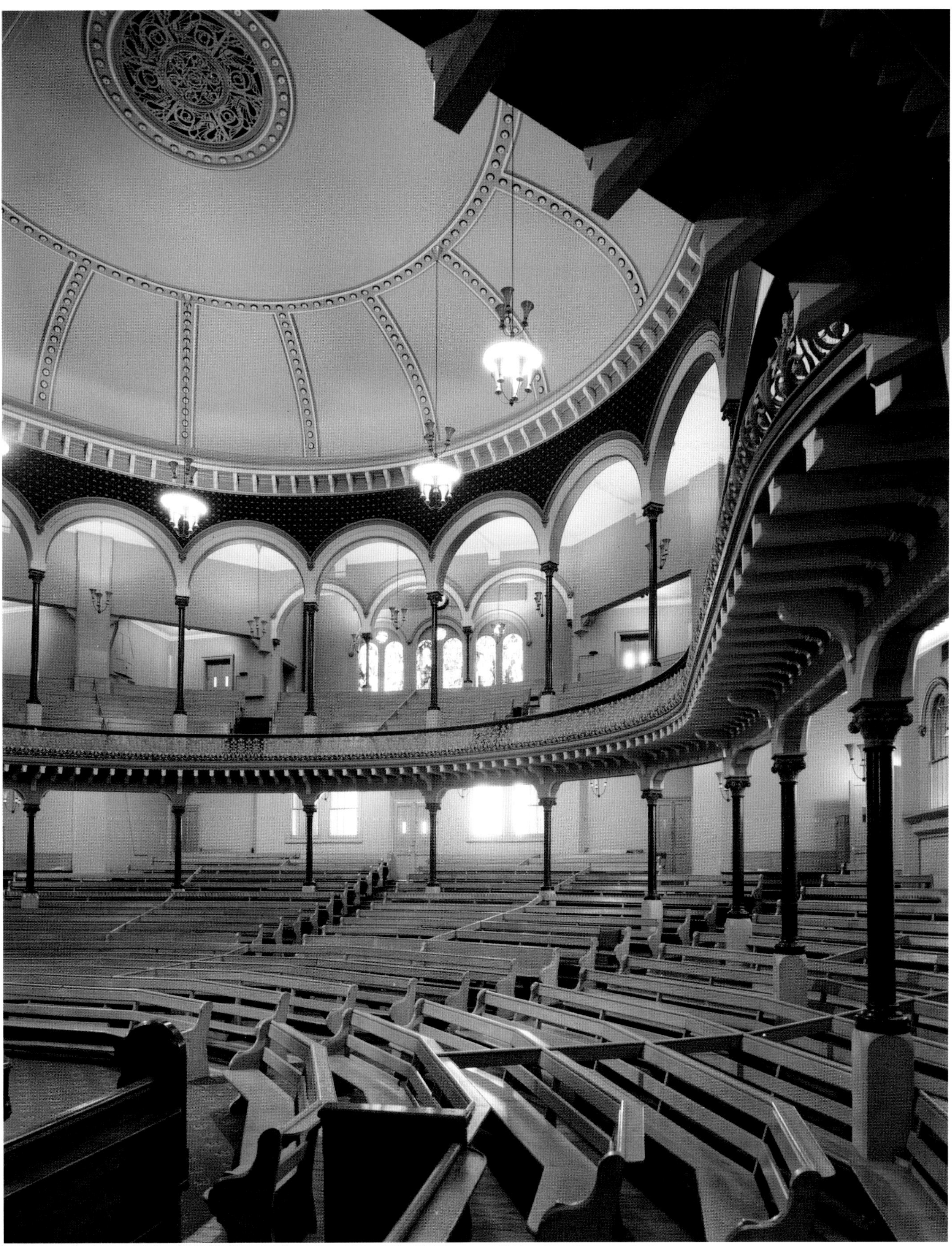

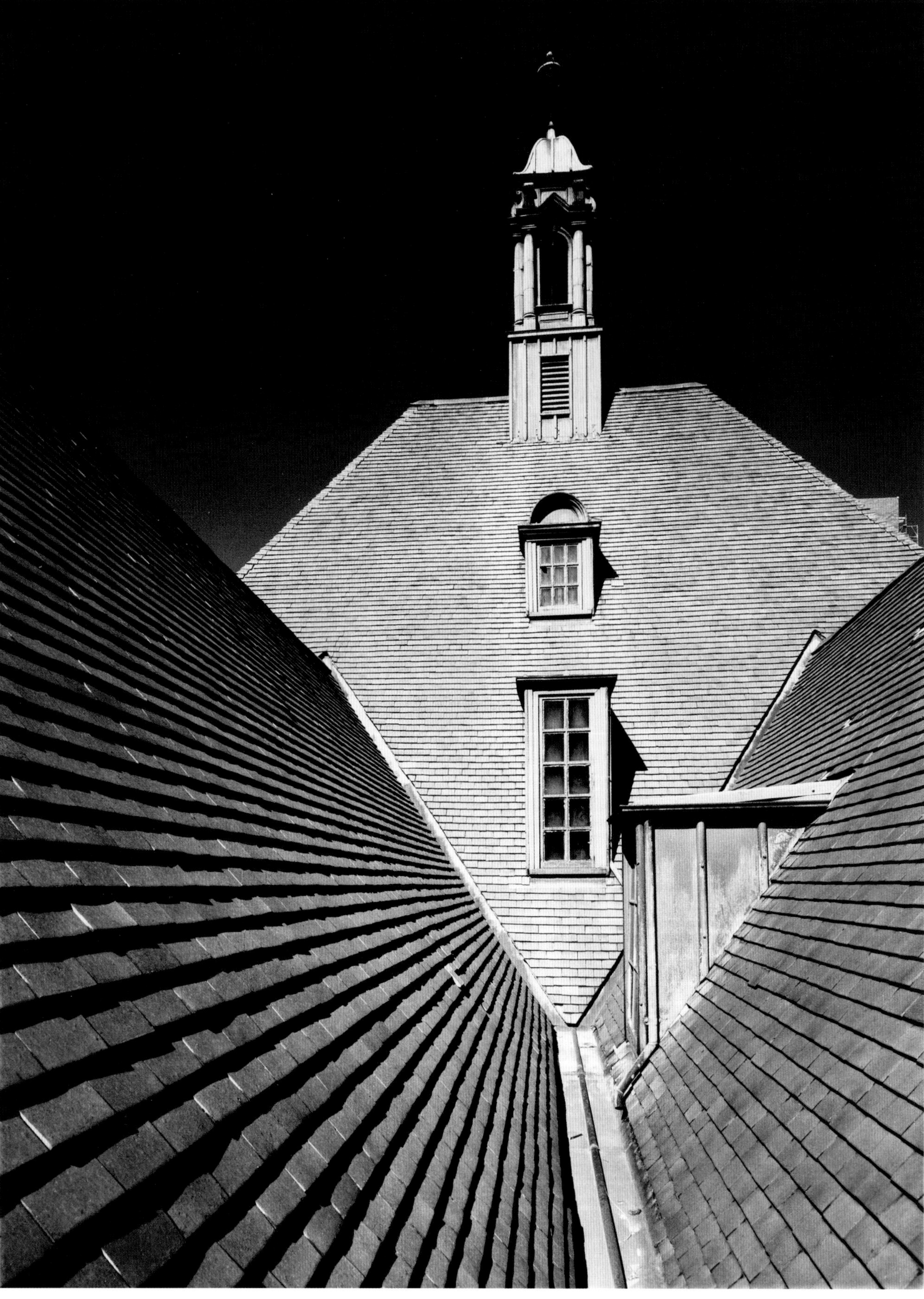

TECHNICAL COMMENTARY

Richard Stringer

LARGE-FORMAT PHOTOGRAPHY

From the outset, I chose to use traditional large-format cameras — the type which needs a tripod and a black cloth, and where the image appears upside down on ground glass at the back. These cameras give you the ability to capture lots of detail and to control perspective. I used Linhof press cameras and, later on, Sinar monorails. They entail more time and effort lugging them around in the field, but in the darkroom life becomes so much easier and rewarding.

These cameras use 5x4 inch sheet film and I chose predominantly Ilford FP3 and FP4. A darkroom was needed to insert each sheet into a film holder. The holder was then slid into the back of the camera to capture the image.

Processing the film was done in deep tanks using Ilford ID11 developer. I could process up to 42 sheets at a time by using acrylic baskets that I built. To control contrast from the great Australian outdoors, the negatives were overexposed and underdeveloped. Nominal development was seven minutes at 20 °C. Ambient temperature in the darkroom would range from 15 °C to 25 °C over the year, which meant varying the processing time to compensate. In summer, it was difficult to maintain even tones across film sheets as development was as short as four minutes.

Printing was undertaken with a Durst Laborator 138S enlarger without a printing frame on the enlarger board. I used the masking blades in the enlarger head to give the image the soft edges that I like. The prints were developed, fixed and washed exactly as recommended in the Ilford Galerie archival printing instructions. I avoided chemicals such as selenium as I did not wish to have any risks with poisons.

Please do not think that all of the foregoing is some sort of ideal procedure. I do not exhaustively test different methodologies. I read books, I speak with people about equipment and processes, decide on something that seems right for me, and then spend my time getting to know it and gaining proficiency. The world has moved on from chemical imagery and I am now learning about digital technology.

DIGITAL PHOTOGRAPHY

The advent of digital photography has brought in new rules. One could capture a lot of information on a sheet of film measuring 5x4 inches. A digital sensor this size would be unaffordable, even if such a thing were on the market. Large images now are mainly achieved by clever computer algorithms. In a strange way, it reinforces my belief that a picture does not have to be big to be good. Less really has become more.

New Zealand Insurance Building 1971, printed 1987

Digital technology has many options and I find that unless I do something constantly, I am forever reaching for the instruction book to discover how I did it a month previously. I have taken to using a Canon EOS 5D camera mainly because, years ago, when I first bought a Canon camera, their servicing was more readily available, so I am now a slave of lock-in.

I use the camera in a conventional way and I still like a tripod. I like stitching images together to obtain larger files and have better satisfaction doing it manually, rather than using any specific computer program. Stitching is facilitated by using a tilt-shift lens. I enjoy the level of control now possible in dealing digitally with tone and colour.

Printing is done using an Epson Stylus Pro 3800 machine with archival inks. Choice of paper varies with availability. As before, I prefer matt surfaces, but the big problem is reliability of supply.

An important requirement now is being able to scan film negatives. I have yet to find something that will scan negatives that are no longer flat due to the ravages of vinegar syndrome. This happens when the cellulose acetate film base of earlier negatives breaks down and distorts in all sorts of ways. I don't think that manufacturers can be bothered with what they see as a limited and vanishing market. Computer editing programs enable some remarkable rescues, albeit needing many labour-intensive hours, provided you get to the damaged images soon enough.

Some of the larger images in this exhibition have been built up by stitching together smaller images. The digital prints of images taken prior to 2007 have been scanned from 120 roll or from 5x4 or 10x8 inch sheet film.

Digital technology also has the advantage of programs that enable quick and flexible searching of extensive image collections.

MOTIVATION

I never intended to be a photographer when I started recording and studying buildings during my days as a student. What prompted me was my dismay when I saw so many worthy structures being demolished and replaced by inferior buildings. I decided that maybe I could make people aware of this by making them look, and the best way I could do this was to put frames around the buildings and hang the images in a place of honour. I could exploit the veracity of photographs if I showed things in the way that they were experienced and without any trickery. I chose to ignore colour in preference for black and white, simply because the photographs lasted better and I could do everything myself.

It was easy enough to identify things at risk and I realised that I would be creating records, so I used a system where you could count every brick. I was impressed by how faithfully buildings had been restored after World War Two, and realised much would have been done with the help of old photographs.

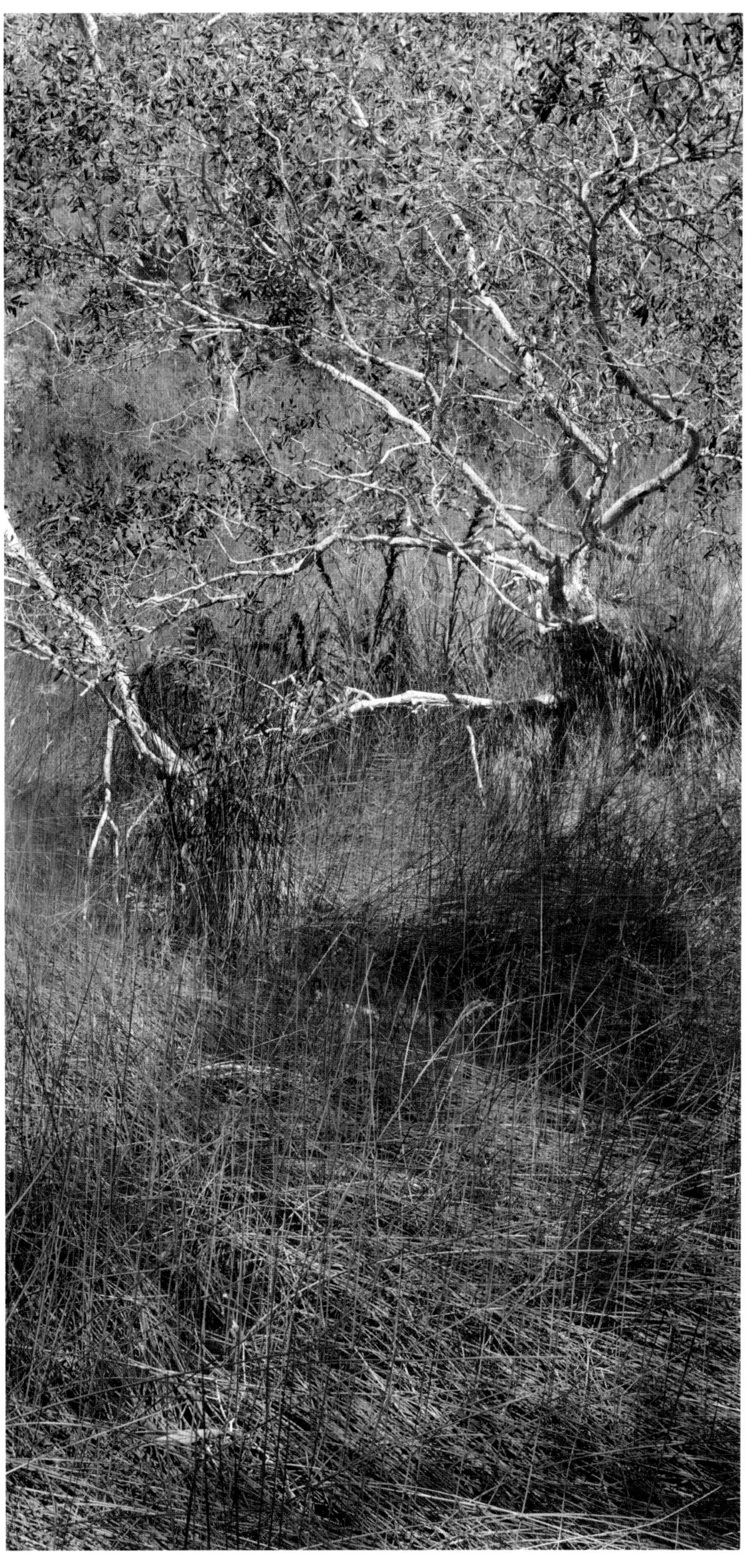

Melaleuca and reeds.
Myora 1989, printed 2013

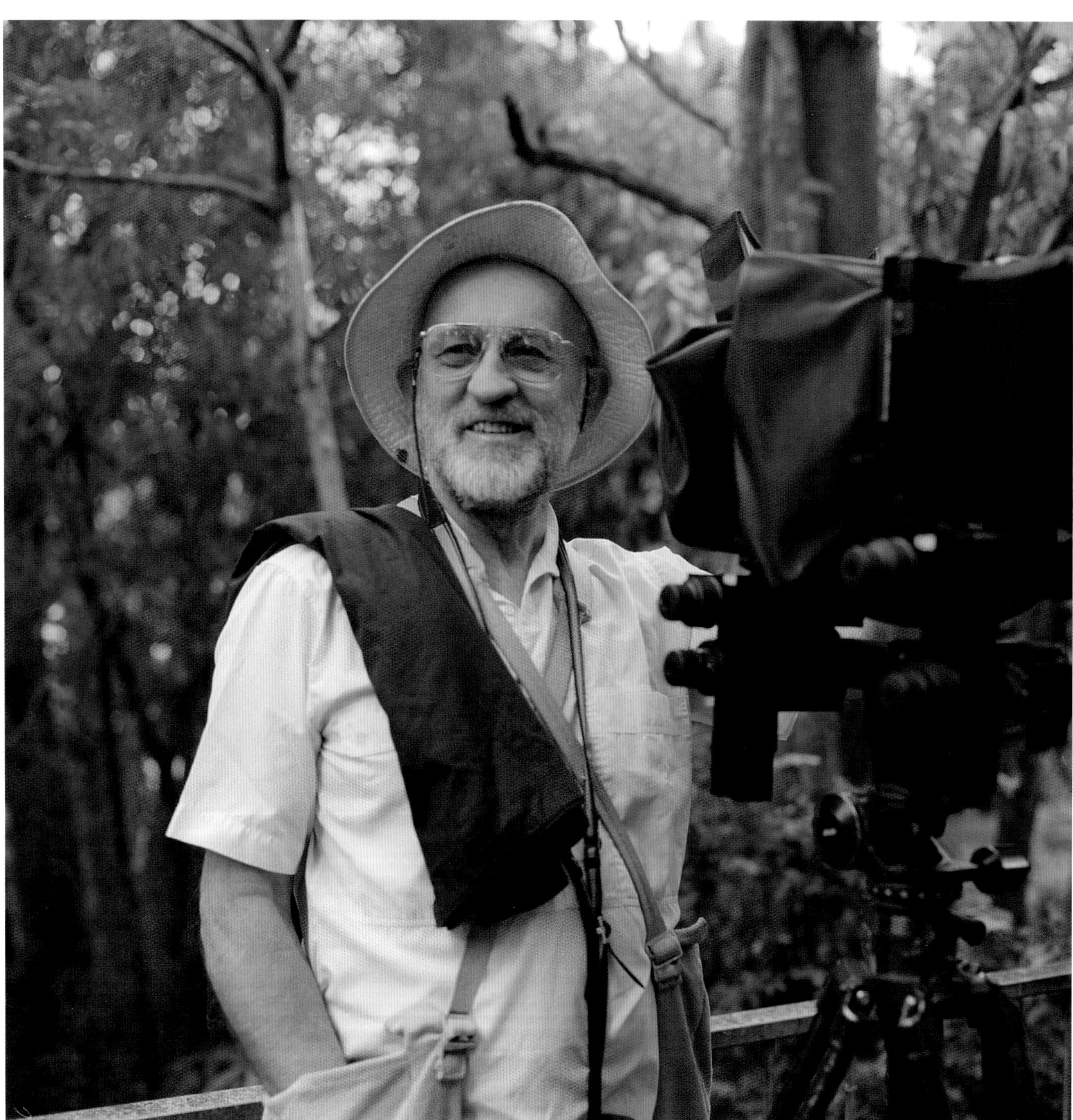

BIOGRAPHY

Richard Stringer was born in Melbourne in 1936. His father was a bank officer and a keen photographer, who documented Australian dance over five decades.[1] In 1960, Stringer graduated from the University of Melbourne with a Bachelor of Architecture, and came to photography through his training and practice as an architect. Moving to Brisbane in 1963, he worked for the renowned architect James Birrell, also a graduate of the University of Melbourne's School of Architecture. In 1967, Stringer set up his own photographic business to document the work of other architects. He later expanded his business with commissions, many notably from the National Trust, to record historic buildings and gardens throughout Queensland and Australia.

Stringer has contributed photographs to a number of significant publications documenting historic sites, including the Australian Council of National Trusts' *Historic Buildings of Australia* series (*Homesteads I* 1969, *Homesteads II* 1976, *Places I* 1978, *Places II* 1979, *Public Buildings* 1971 and *Houses* 1974), *Building Queensland's Heritage* 1978, *Historic Homes of Brisbane: A Selection* 1979 and *Living History of Brisbane* 1982; Howard Tanner's exhibition catalogue *The Art of Gardening in Colonial Australia: Converting the Wilderness* 1979, *Architects of Australia* 1981 and *Towards an Australian Garden* 1983; John Millington and Mark Rigby's *John Rigby: Art and Life* 2003; Robert Riddel's *Robin Dods, 1868–1920: Selected Works* 2012; and, with his wife Marguerite Stringer (who contributed the text), *A Shifting Town: Glass-Plate Images of Clermont and its People by GC Pullar* 1986.

Stringer has taught photography for many years, including at the Faculty of Architecture, University of Queensland (1964–70), and at the Queensland College of Art (1979–88, 1991–92, 2002). He has also recorded the majority of exhibitions at Brisbane's Institute of Modern Art (IMA) since 1976 — in 1984, he was made an honorary life member of the IMA — and has documented numerous exhibitions at the Queensland Art Gallery. In 2002, Stringer was made a Fellow of the Royal Australian Institute of Architects, and he received an Honorary Doctorate of Philosophy from the University of Queensland in 2003.

He has held a number of solo exhibitions and participated in many group showings. Solo exhibitions have included 'Fretwork Pediments in Queensland', University of Queensland Art Museum, 1982; 'Photographs by Richard Stringer', Bellas Gallery, Brisbane, 1987 and 1988; 'Queensland Remembers: War Memorials: Photographs by Richard Stringer', Queensland Museum, Brisbane, 1995; 'Vanishing Queensland: Photographs by Richard Stringer', a National Trust of Queensland and Regional Galleries Association of Queensland touring exhibition, 2000; and 'The Blair Pavilion: Photographs by Richard Stringer', Ipswich Art Gallery, 2009. Richard Stringer's photographs are held in state and national collections, including the National Library of Australia and Parliament House, Canberra; National Gallery of Victoria, Melbourne; Ipswich Art Gallery; and the University of Queensland and the Queensland Art Gallery, Brisbane.

Richard Stringer, 1999
Photograph: Marguerite Stringer

Endnote

1 The WF Stringer Collection is held by the National Library of Australia, Canberra.

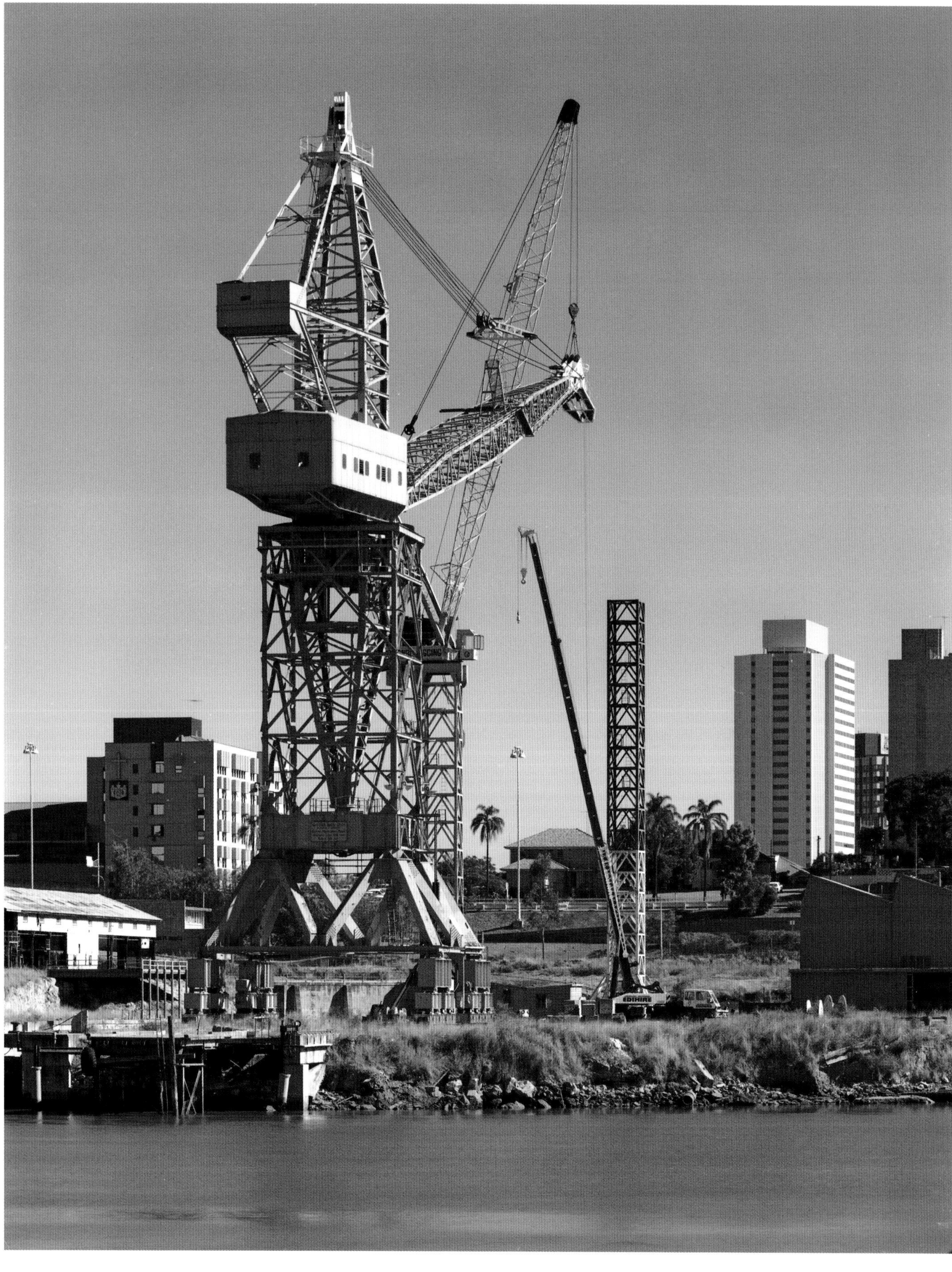

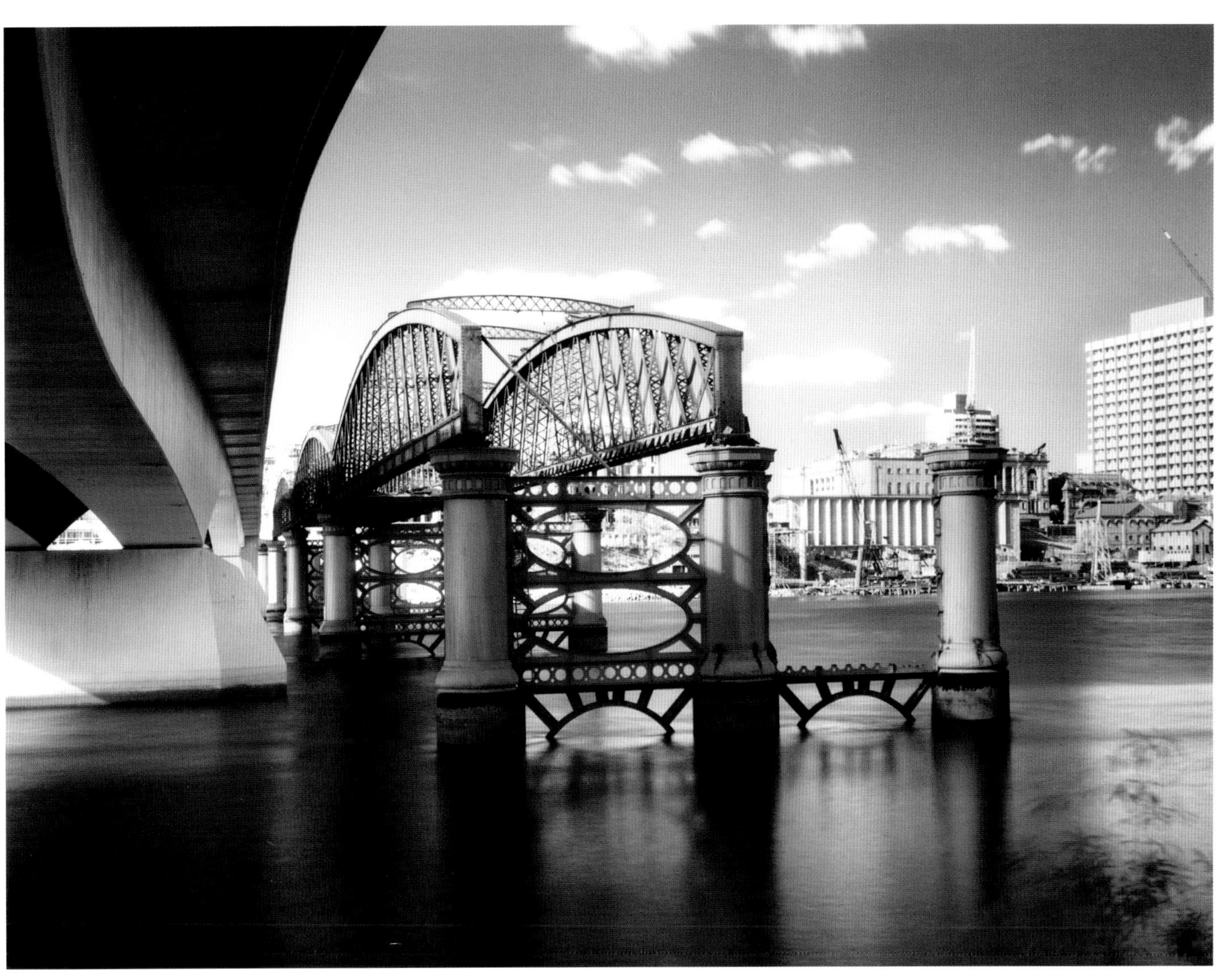

Victoria Bridges 5 & 4
1970, printed 2013

Opposite: *The big crane, Evans Deakin Shipyard* 1979, printed 2013

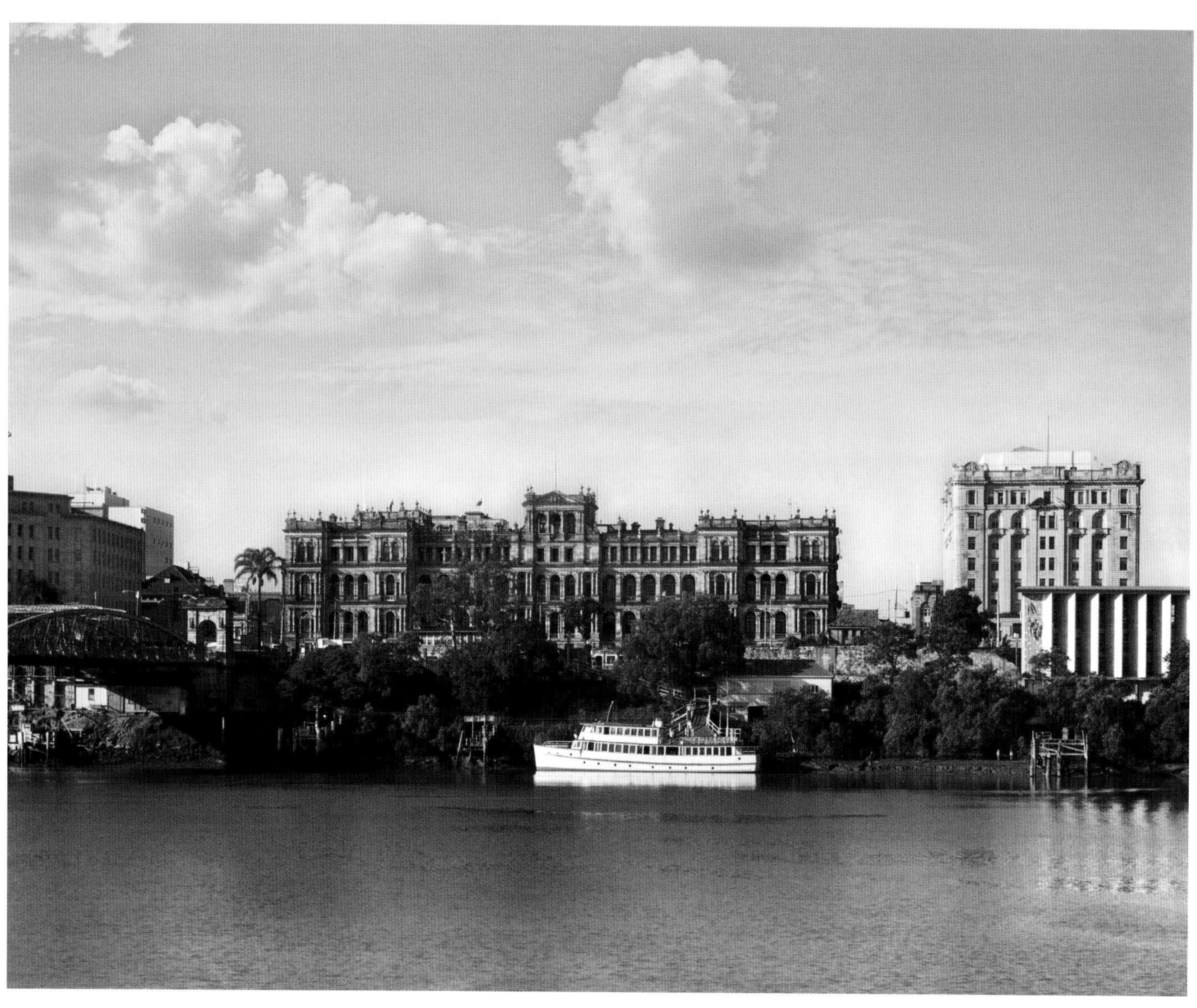

Treasury Building, Brisbane
1967, printed 2013

Opposite: *Final call of the dredge 'Brisbane'* 1989, printed 2013

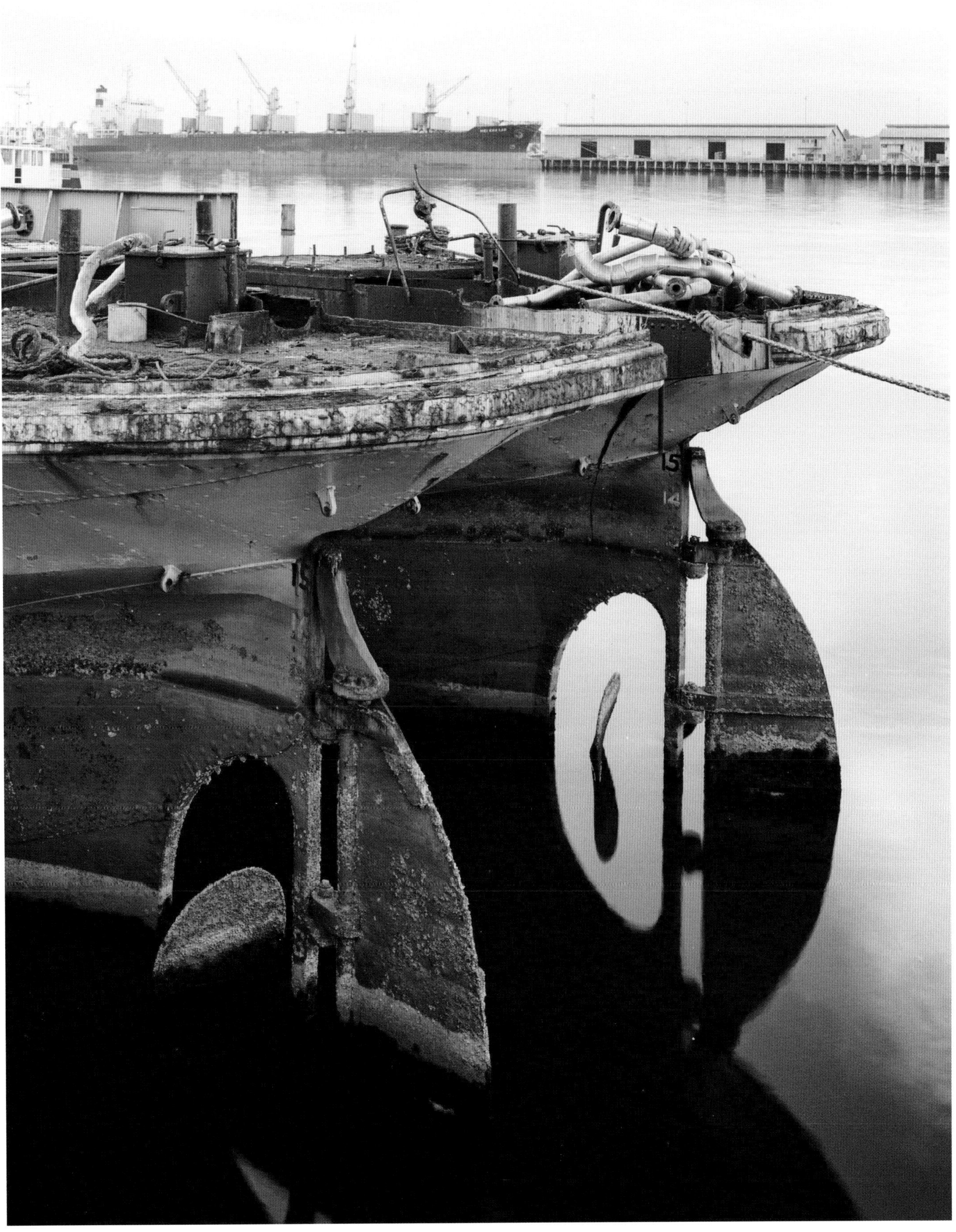

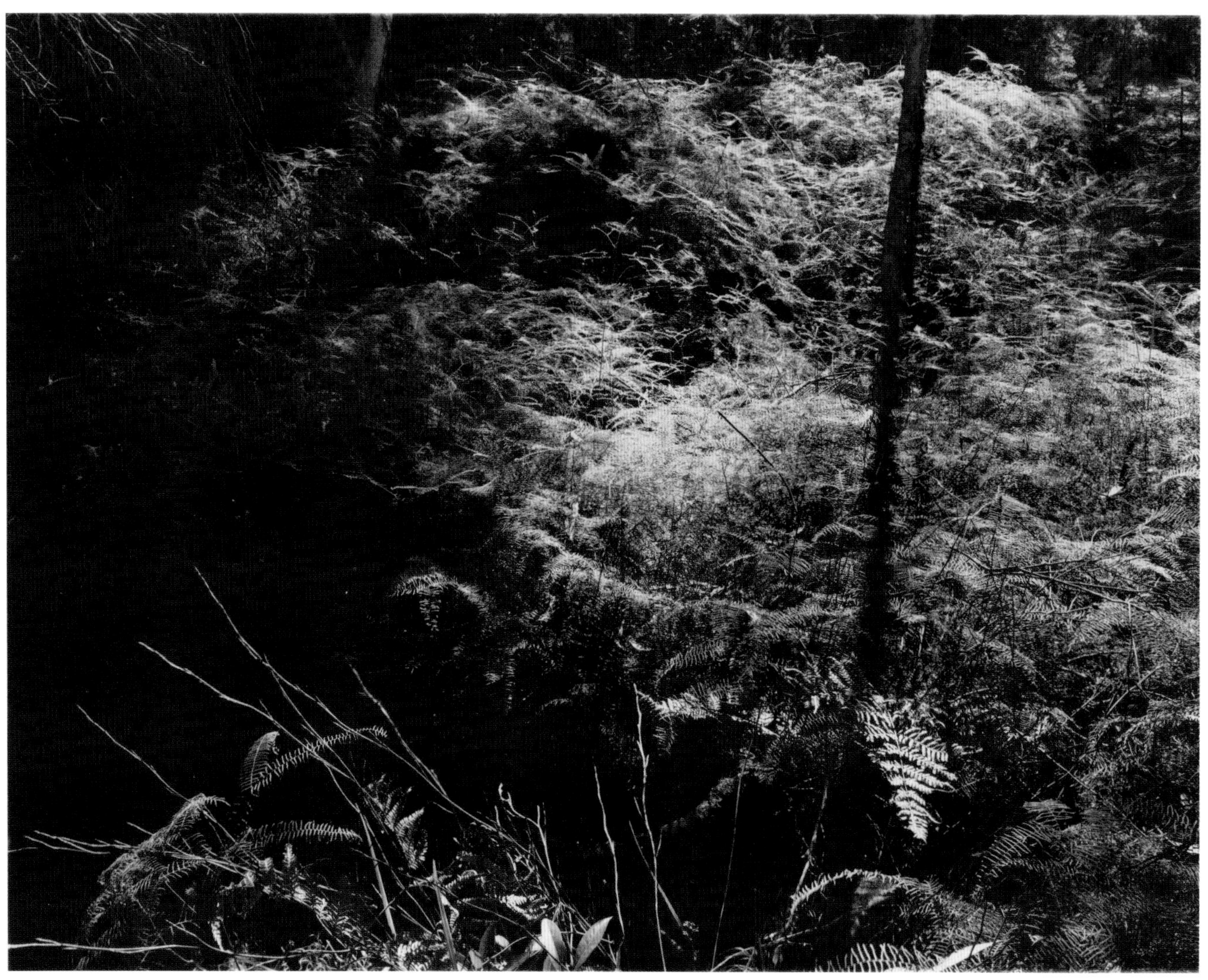

Myora fern 1985, printed 1987

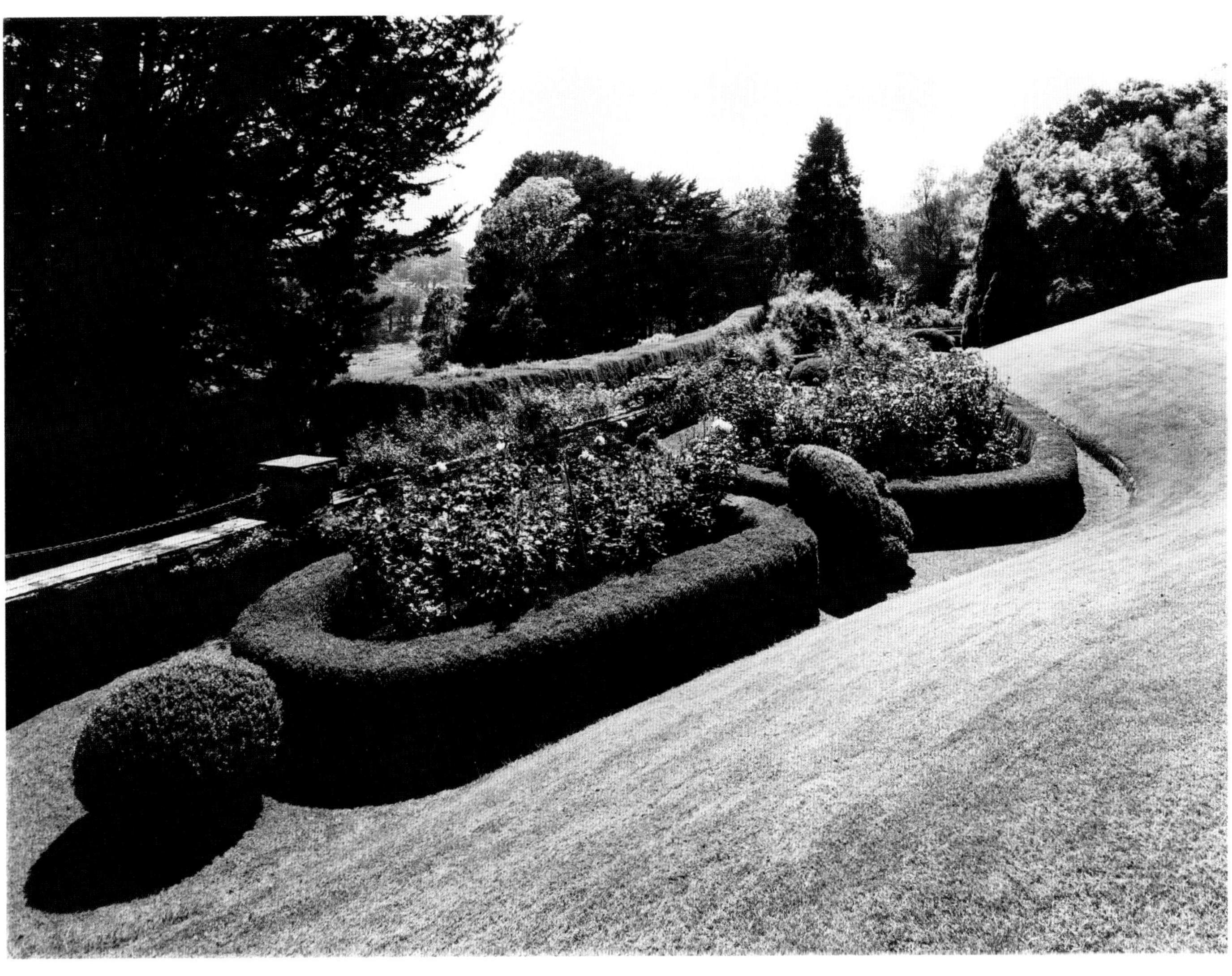

Milton Park 1981, printed 1987

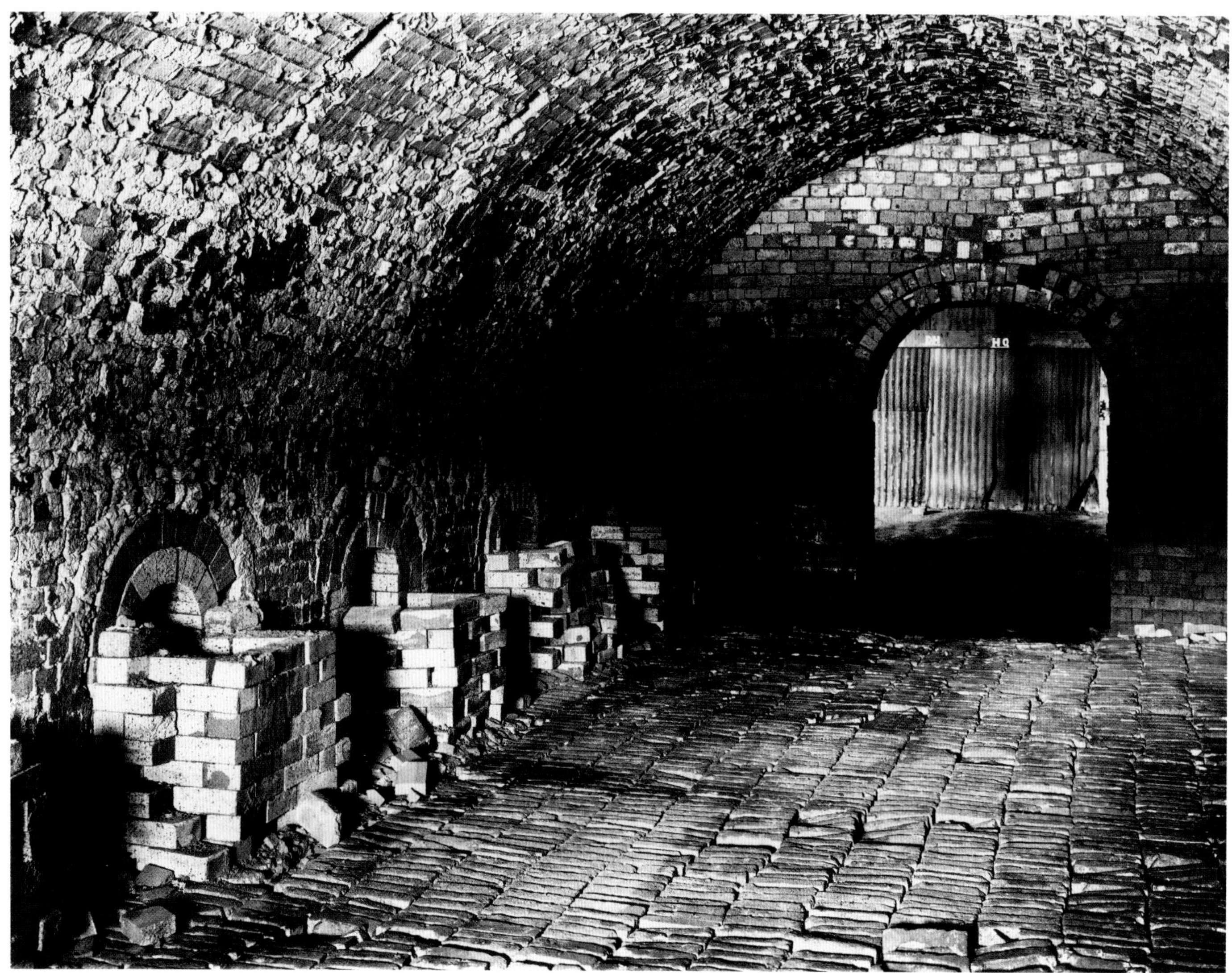

Dinmore Pottery 1984, printed 1987

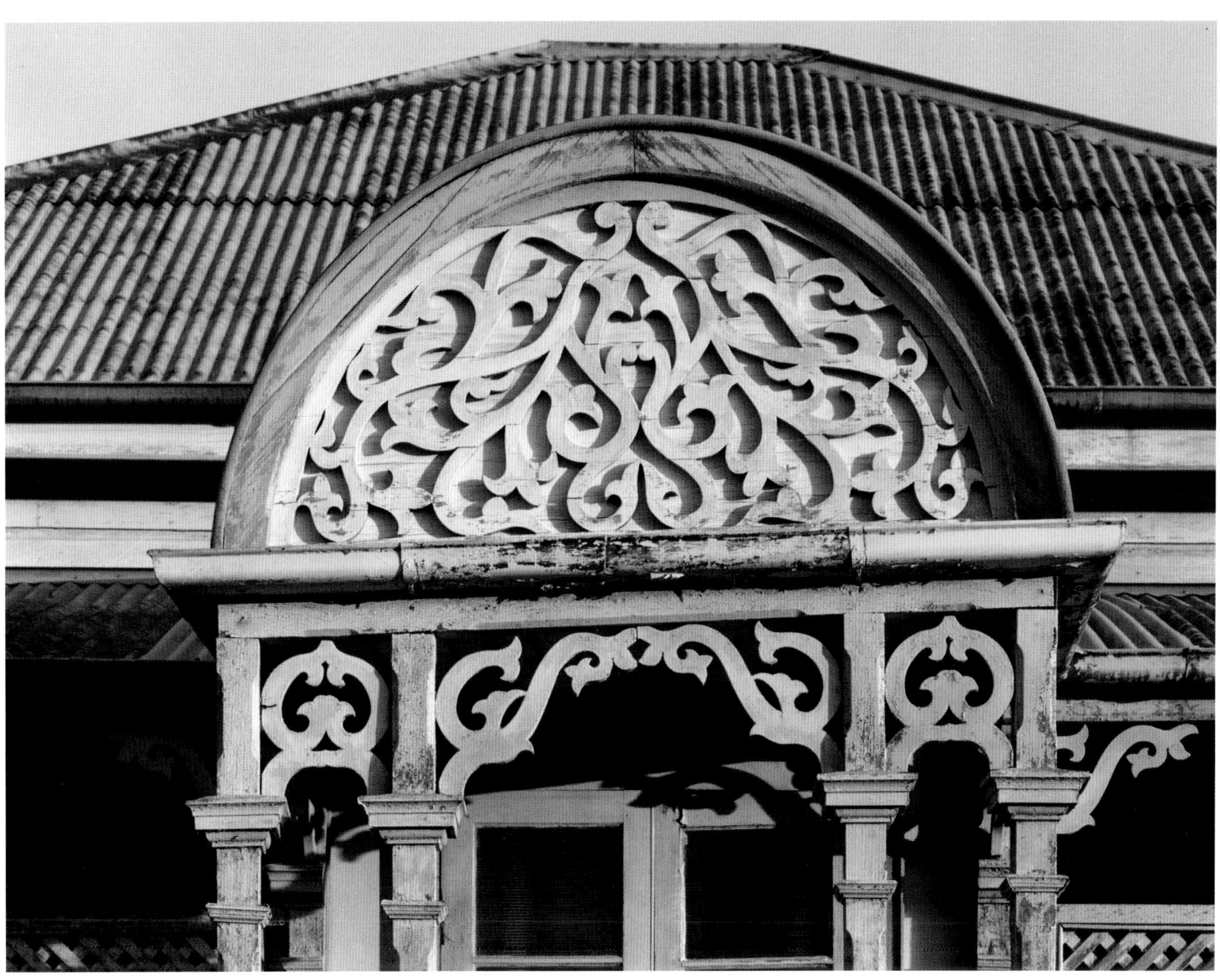

Timber fret panel, Bundaberg
1987, printed 2013

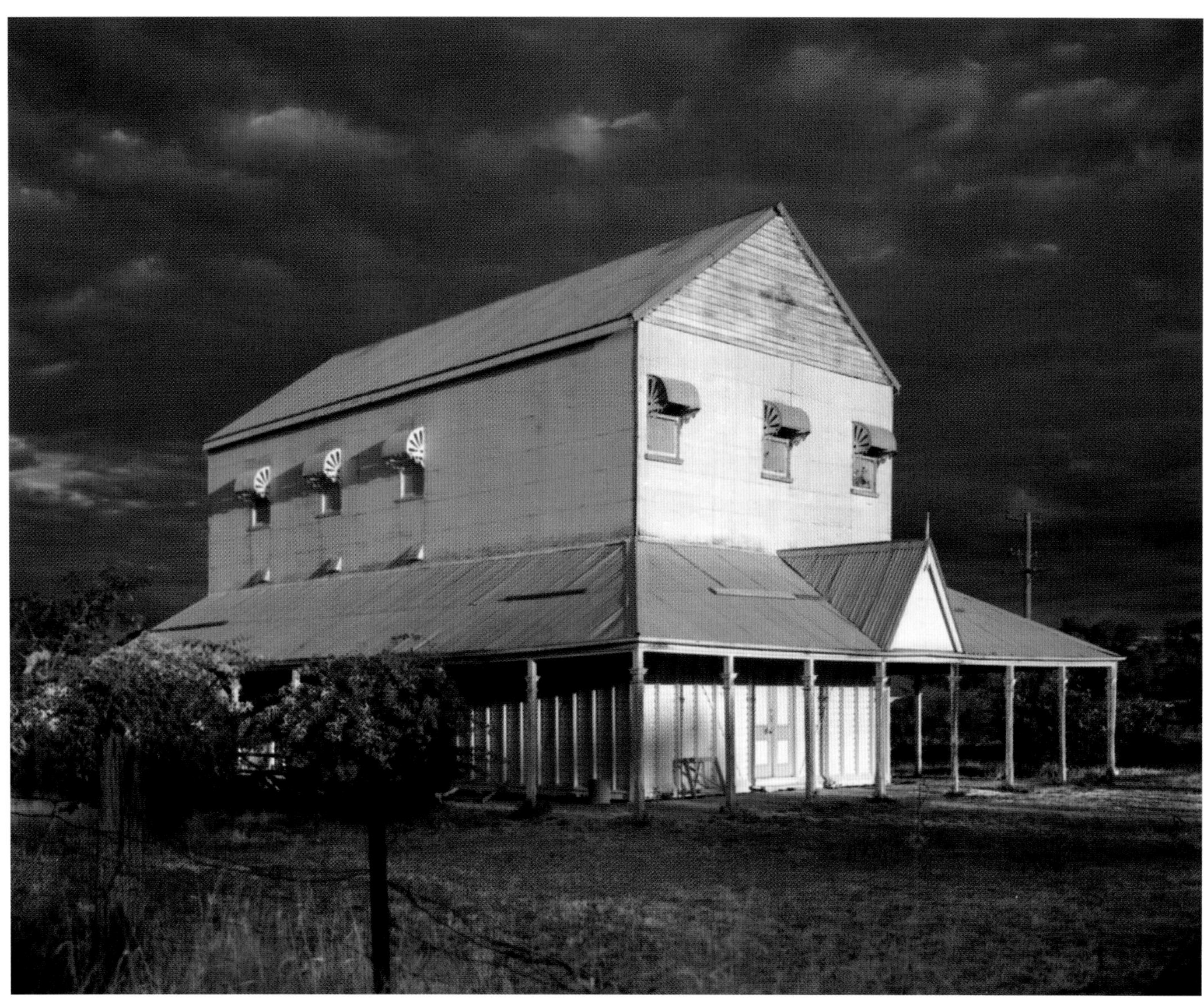

Blackall Masonic Lodge
1975, printed 2013

Opposite: *Interior, Boggo Road Gaol* 1992, printed 2013

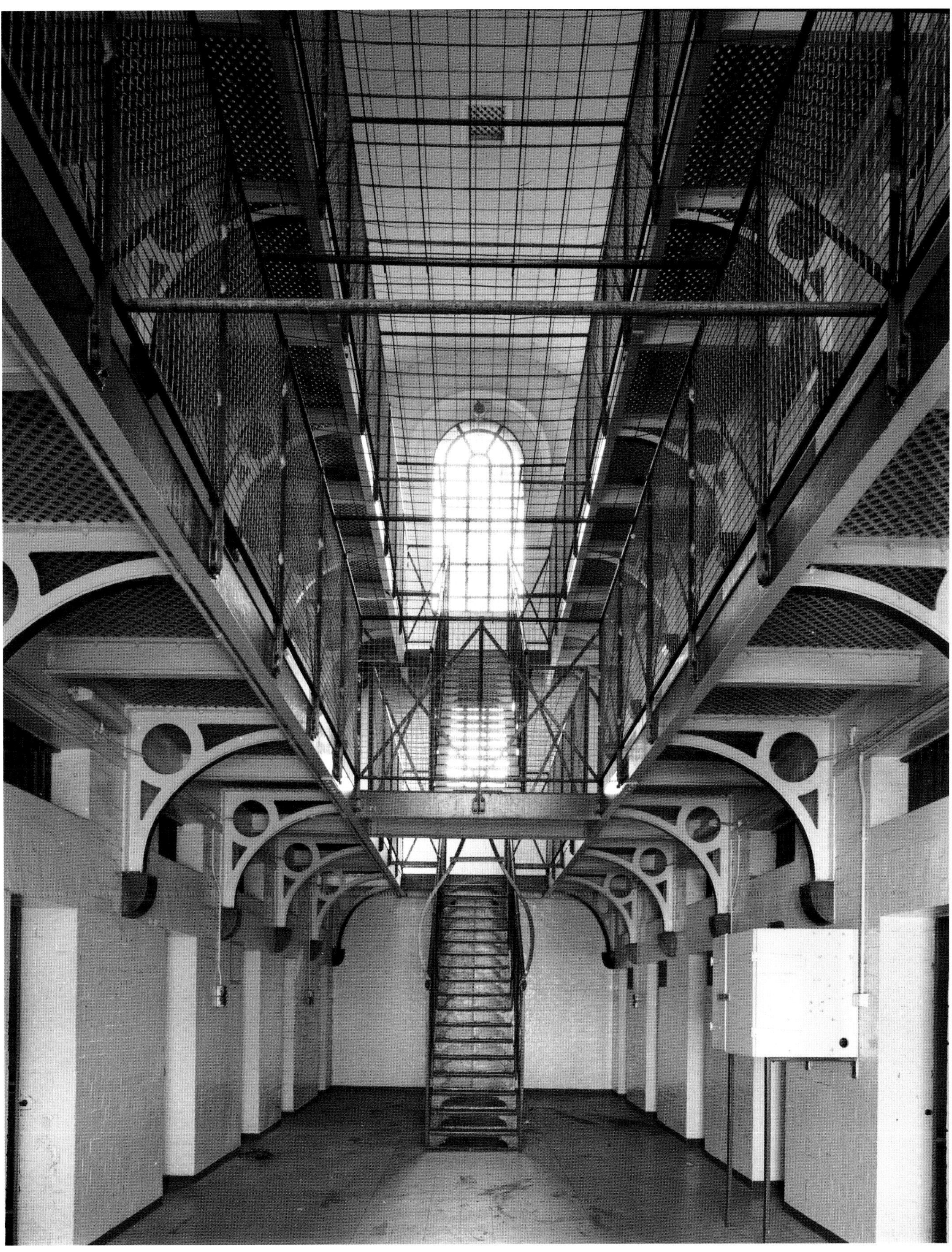

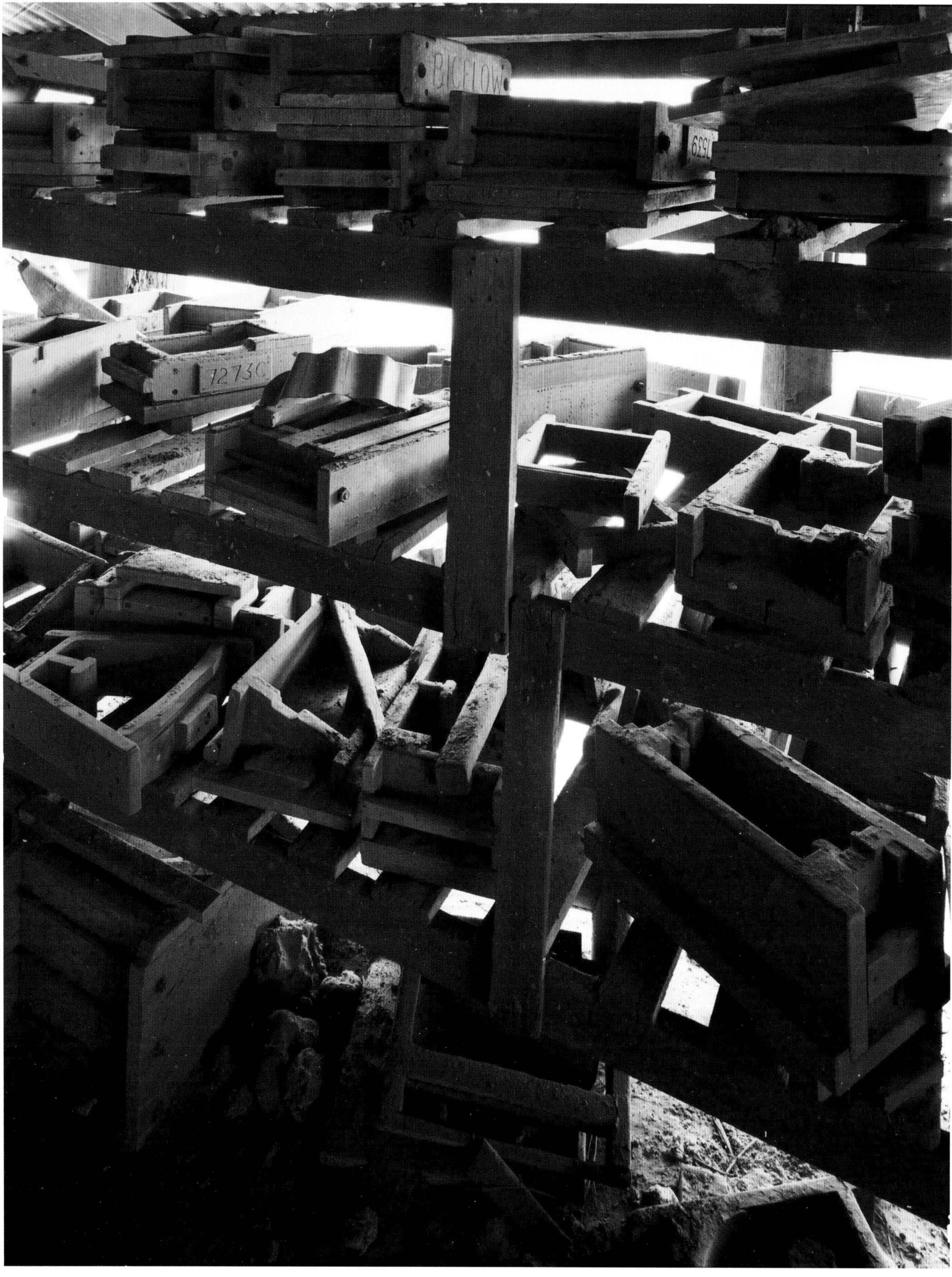
BIGELOW
1273C

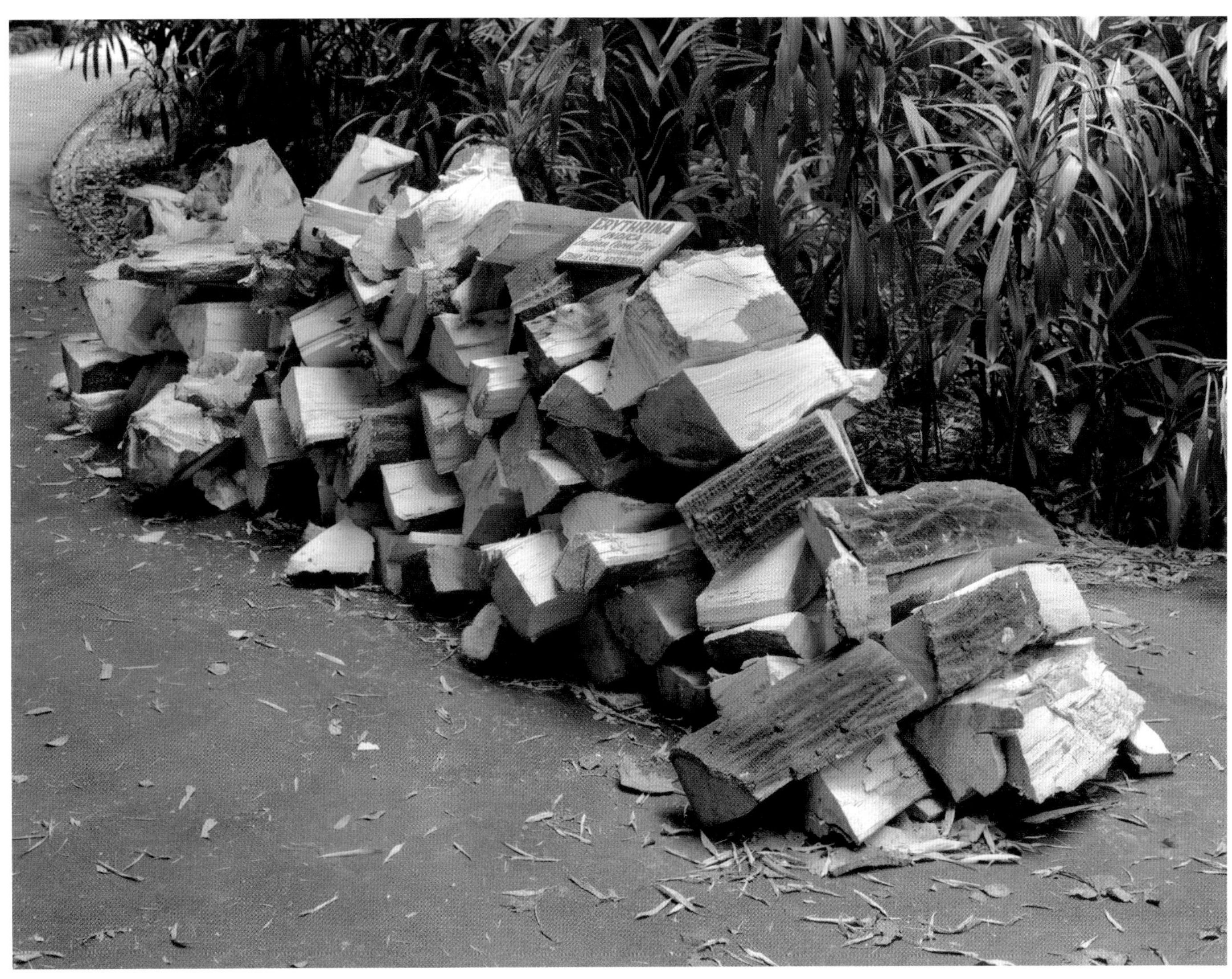

Taxonomy, Royal Botanic Gardens, Melbourne 1982, printed 2013

Opposite: *Casting boxes, Rylance Brickworks* 1991, printed 2013

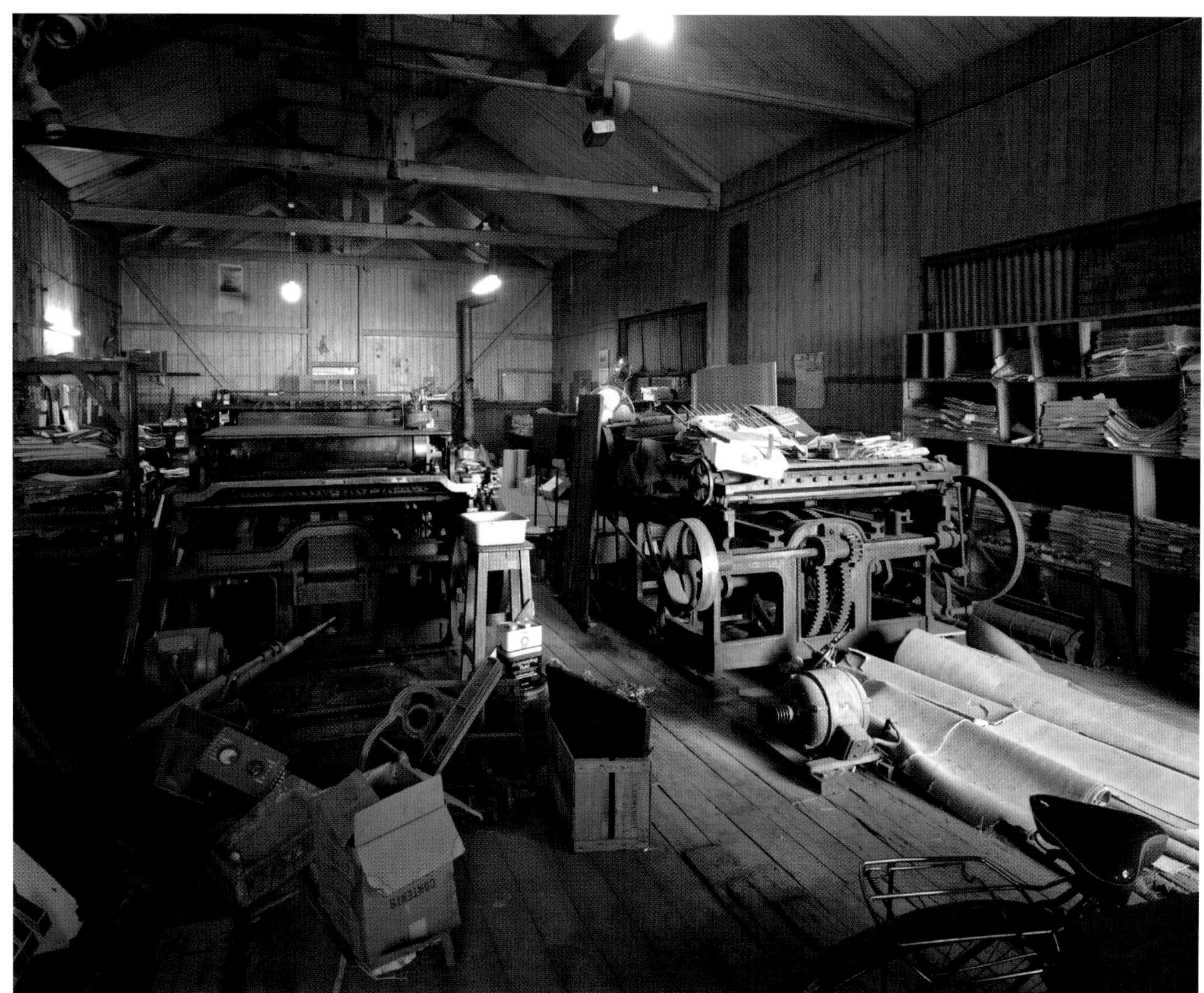

The Western Star,
Roma 1982, printed 2013

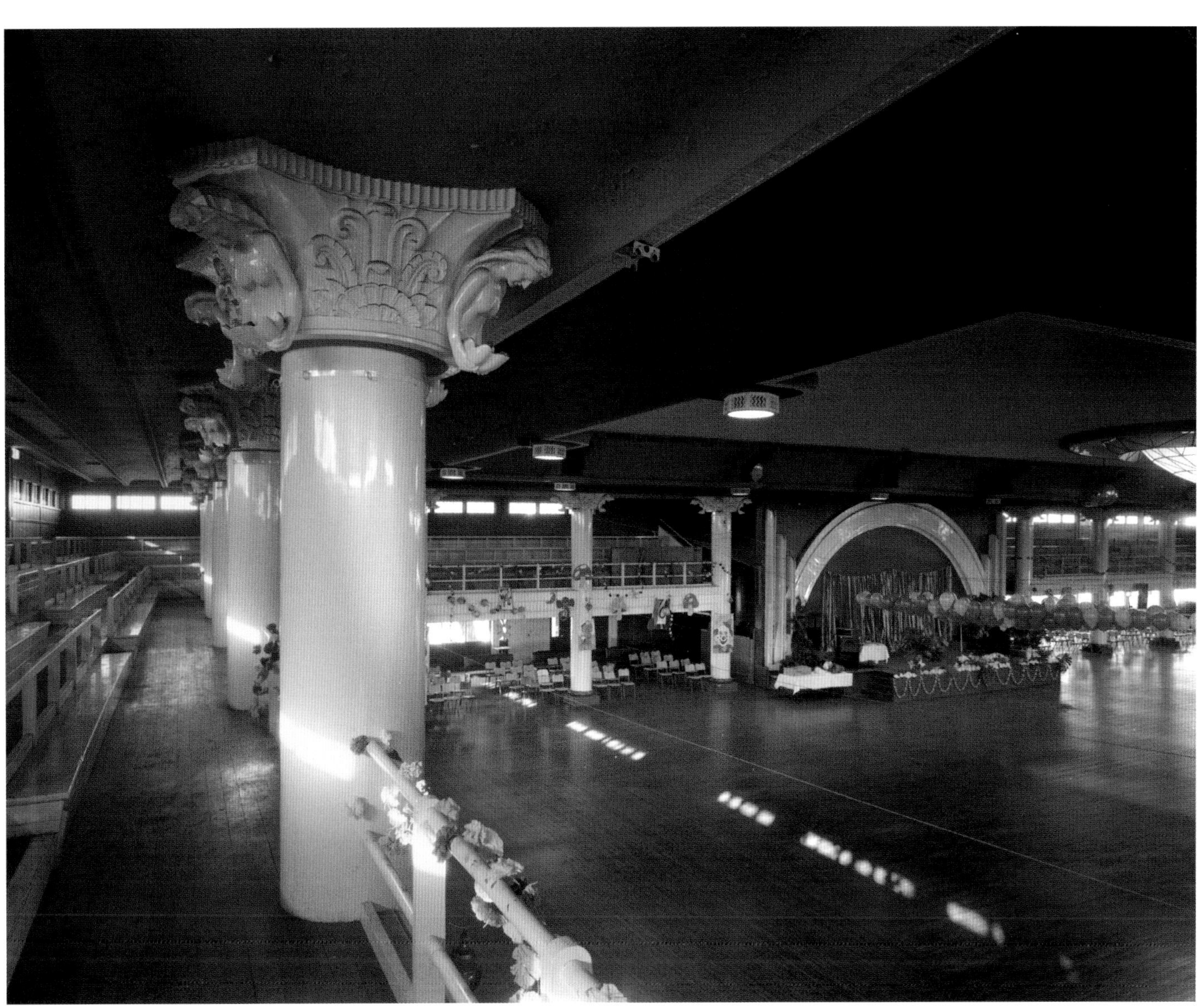

Interior, Cloudland Ballroom, Bowen Hills 1982, printed 2013

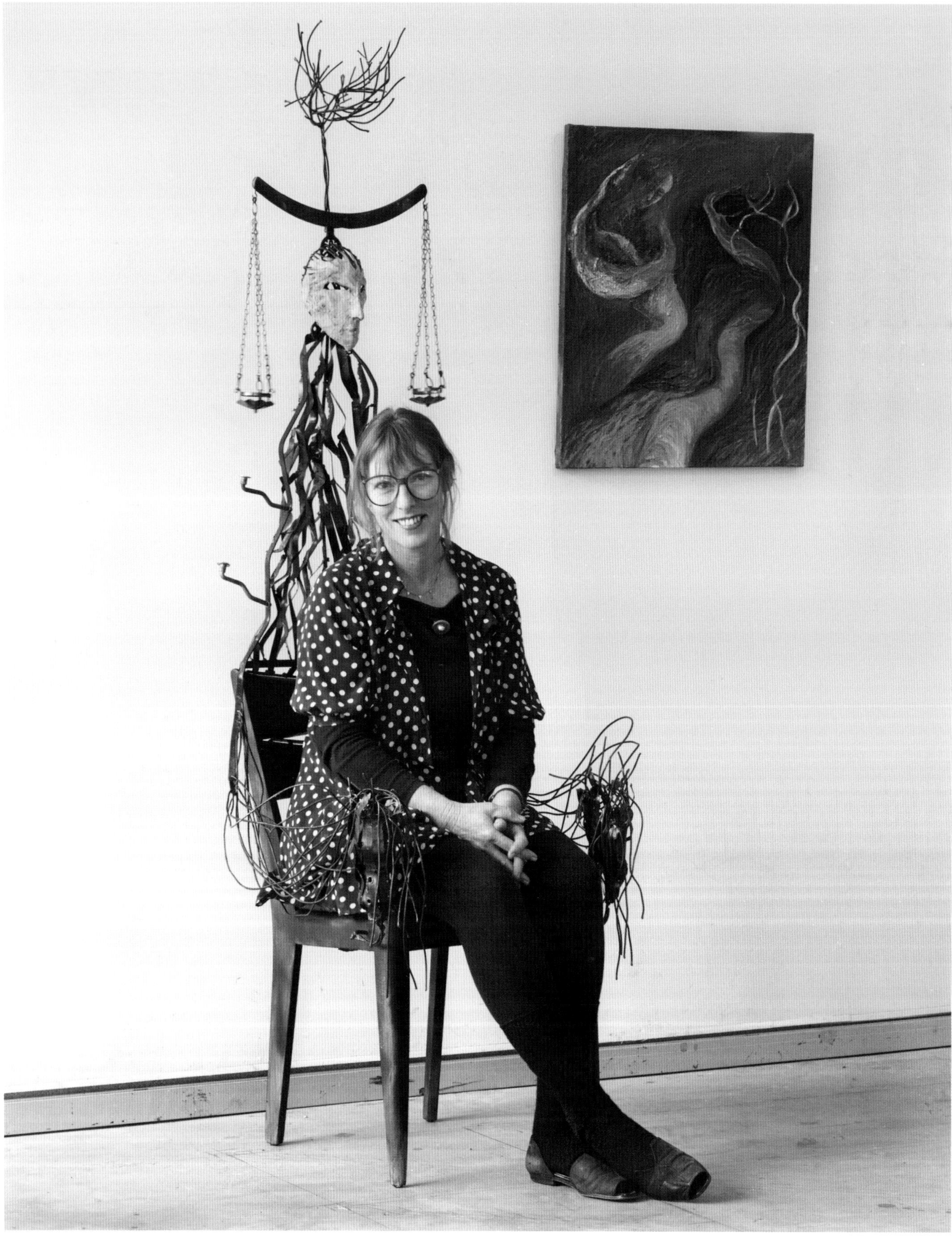

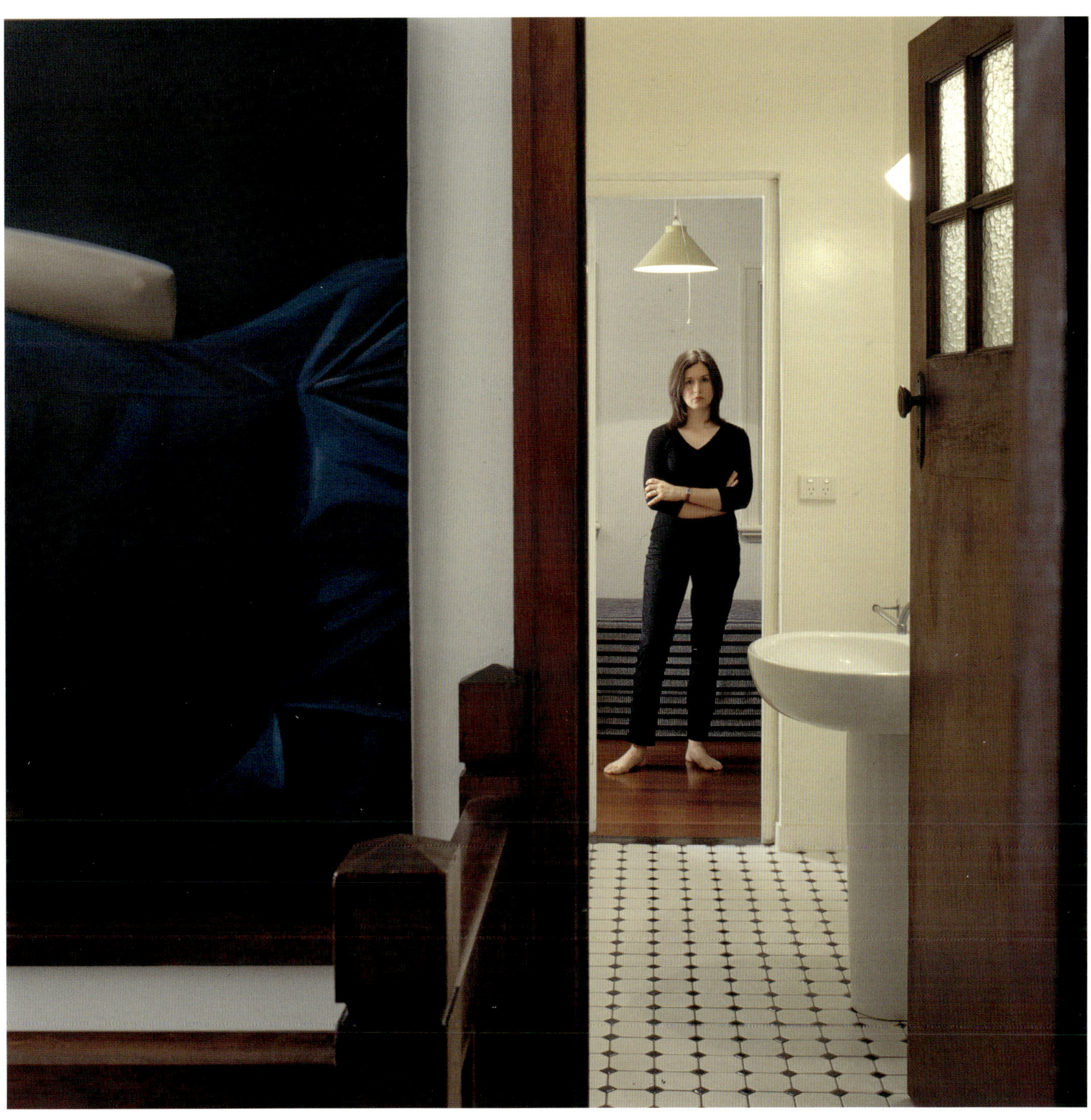

Anne Wallace 2004, printed 2013

Opposite: *Mona Ryder* 1990, printed 2013

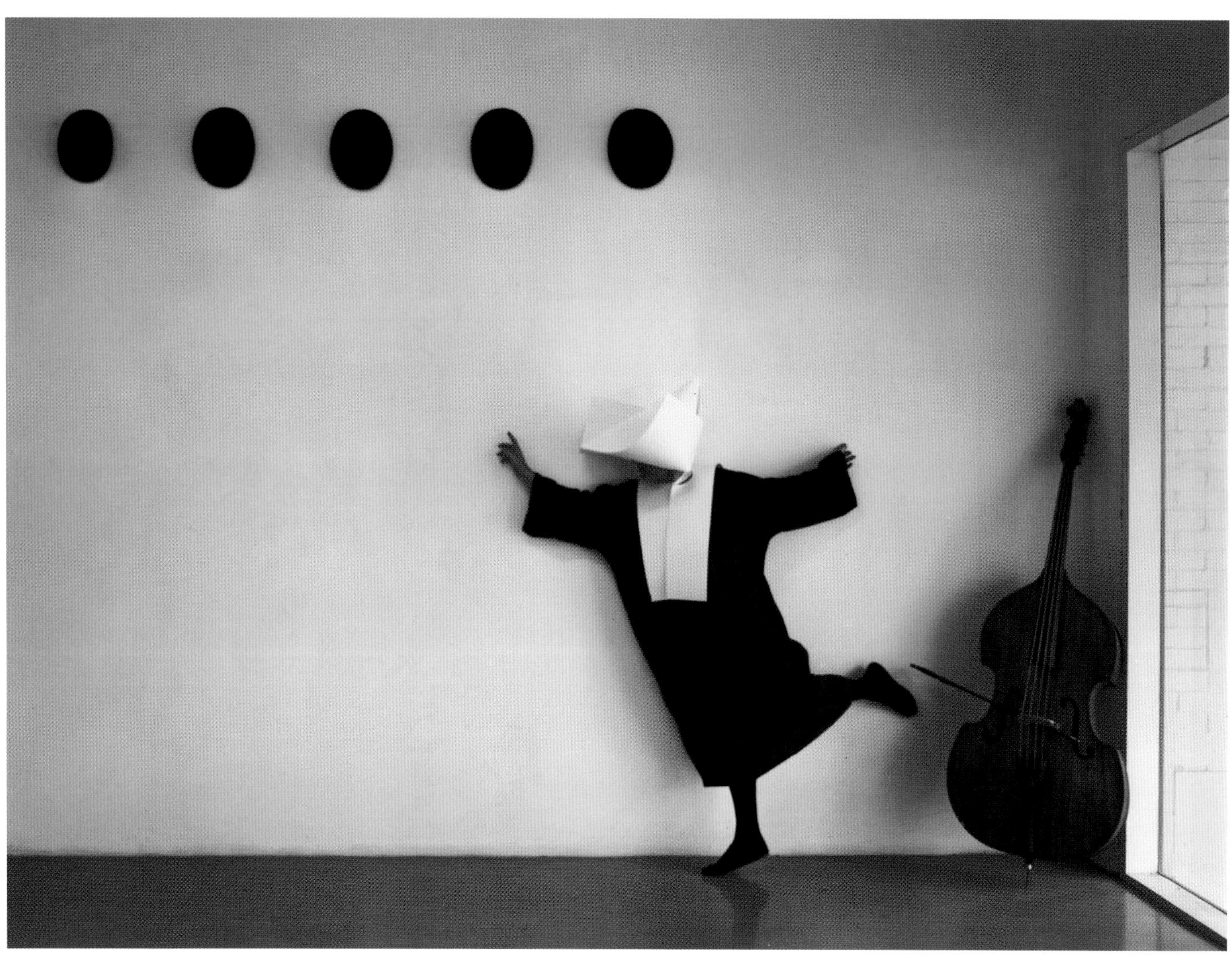

Luke Roberts, Bellas Gallery 1988, printed 2013

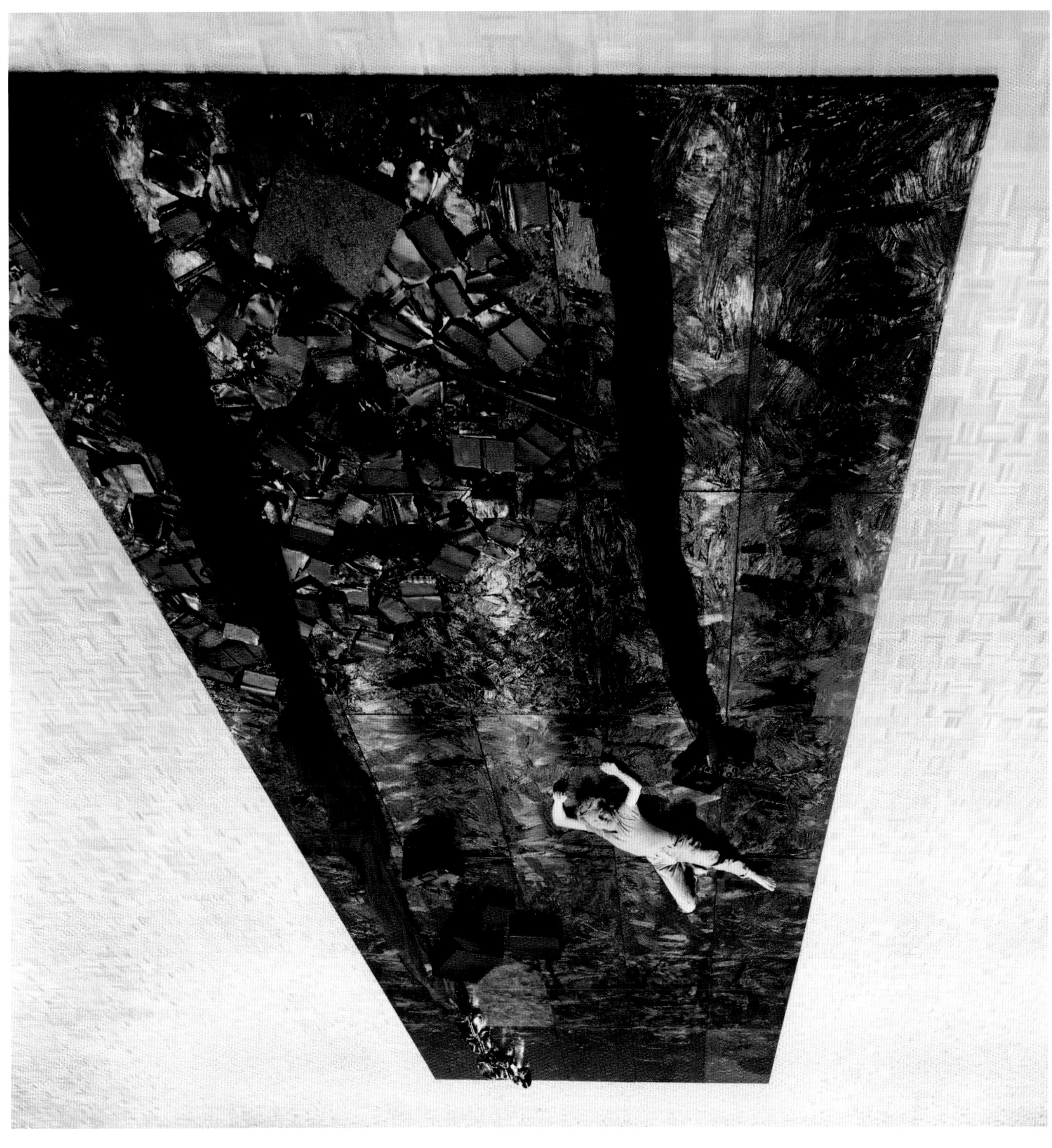

The apotheosis of Scott Redford 1987, printed 2013

CATALOGUE OF WORKS

Works are listed in chronological order. Dimensions are given in centimetres (cm), height preceding width, followed by depth. Unless otherwise indicated, dimensions refer to paper size. Page numbers of works reproduced in this publication are indicated.

*The art works indicated with an asterisk (*) are proposed gifts to the Queensland Art Gallery Collection from the artist.

Richard Stringer
Australia b.1936

Before the service station, Charters Towers 1966, printed 2013*
Digital print / 42 x 59.5cm / p.28

Church at Gatton 1967, printed 2013*
Digital print / 42 x 29.5cm / p.27

Gravel deliveries, South Brisbane 1967, printed 2013*
Digital print / 59.5 x 42cm / p.6

Placing a sail unit, Sydney Opera House 1967, printed 2013*
Digital print / 59.5 x 42cm / p.15

Treasury Building, Brisbane 1967, printed 2013*
Digital print / 42 x 59.5cm / p.40

Brampton Island Airport 1968, printed 2013*
Digital print / 42 x 59.5cm / p.24

Curtain raiser, Bellevue precinct, Brisbane 1968, printed 2013*
Digital print / 42 x 59.5cm / p.18

Railway Station, Rockhampton 1969, printed 2013
Digital print / 42 x 59.5cm / Collection: The artist

Morning on St Paul's Terrace 1970, printed 2013*
Digital print / 42 x 59.5cm / p.30

Victoria Bridges 5 & 4 1970, printed 2013*
Digital print / 42 x 59.5cm / p.39

New Zealand Insurance Building 1971, printed 1987
Gelatin silver photograph / 42 x 31cm (comp.) / Purchased 1987 / Collection: Queensland Art Gallery / p.32

Variations on Normanton Railway Station 1971
Toned gelatin silver print / Four panels: 51 x 40.5cm (each) / Collection: The artist

Thursday Island Cemetery 1973, printed 2013
Digital print / 59.5 x 42cm / Collection: The artist

Australia Day flood 1974, printed 1987
Gelatin silver photograph / 30.6 x 41cm (comp.) / Purchased 1987 / Collection: Queensland Art Gallery

Breezeway, Yengarie Sugar Mill 1974, printed 2013*
Digital print / 59.5 x 42cm / p.8

Memory of the Bellevue 1974–79
Toned gelatin silver print with wood, brick, glass / 31.2 x 35cm (framed) / Collection: The artist

Blackall Masonic Lodge 1975, printed 2013*
Digital print / 42 x 59.5cm / p.46

Cornice, Regent Theatre, Brisbane 1975, printed 2013
Digital print / 59.5 x 42cm / Collection: The artist / p.12

Manager's house, Ilfracombe Wool Scour 1975, printed 2013
Digital print / 42 x 59.5cm / Collection: The artist / p.14

November, Maryborough Cemetery 1975, printed 2013
Digital print / 42 x 59.5cm / Collection: The artist

Slag blockwork, Mt Chalmers Copper and Gold Mine 1975, printed 2013
Digital print / 42 x 59.5cm / Collection: The artist / p.22

Interior, Geraghty's Grocery, Maryborough 1976, printed 2013*
Digital print / 42 x 59.5cm

Congregational Church, New Town, Tasmania 1977, printed 2013
Digital print / 59.5 x 42cm / Collection: The artist

Goats, St Helena Prison 1977, printed 2013*
Digital print / 42 x 59.5cm / cover

Independent Church, Melbourne 1977, printed 2013
Digital print / 59.5 x 42cm / Collection: The artist / p.31

Salter residence, Toorak 1977, printed 2013
Digital print / 42 x 59.5cm / Collection: The artist

Boatshed, Ripponlea 1978, printed 1985
Gelatin silver photograph / 32 x 41.8cm (comp.) / Purchased 1987 / Collection: Queensland Art Gallery

View of Brisbane from South Brisbane 1978, printed 2013
Digital print / 42 x 59.5cm / Collection: The artist

The big crane, Evans Deakin Shipyard 1979, printed 2013
Digital print / 59.5 x 42cm / Collection: The artist / p.38

Andrew Petrie stonemasons 1980, printed 1987
Gelatin silver photograph / 31.5 x 41.8cm (comp.) / Purchased 1987 / Collection: Queensland Art Gallery

Queensland Cultural Centre construction 1980, printed 2013
Digital print / 65.3 x 118.9cm / Collection: The artist

Milton Park 1981, printed 1987
Gelatin silver photograph / 31.4 x 42cm (comp.) / Purchased 1987 / Collection: Queensland Art Gallery / p.43

Tomb of John Macarthur, Camden Park 1981, printed 2013
Digital print / 42 x 59.5cm / Collection: The artist

Gum trees, Mount Emu Creek 1982, printed 2013*
Digital print / 42 x 59.5cm / p.23

House, Roma 1982, printed 1987
Gelatin silver photograph / 31.5 x 41.7cm (comp.) / Purchased 1987 / Collection: Queensland Art Gallery / p.16

Interior, Cloudland Ballroom, Bowen Hills 1982, printed 2013*
Digital print / 42 x 59.5cm / p.51

'Killymoon', Tasmania 1982, printed 2013
Digital print / 42 x 59.5cm / Collection: The artist

Queensland Art Gallery Watermall 1982, printed 2013*
Digital print / 42 x 59.5cm / p.10

Take me to your leader, confined space piling 1982, printed 2013
Digital print / 42 x 59.5cm / Collection: The artist

Taxonomy, Royal Botanic Gardens, Melbourne 1982, printed 2013
Digital print / 42 x 59.5cm / Collection: The artist / p.49

The Western Star, Roma 1982, printed 2013
Digital print / 42 x 59.5cm / Collection: The artist / p.50

Clay storage shed, Dinmore Pottery 1984, printed 2013
Digital print / 42 x 59.5cm / Collection: The artist

Dinmore Pottery 1984, printed 1987
Gelatin silver photograph / 31.5 x 41.7cm (comp.) / Purchased 1987 / Collection: Queensland Art Gallery / p.44

Red Comb House 1984, printed 2013
Digital print / 42 x 59.5cm / Collection: The artist

Government Printer's Office, George Street 1985, printed 2013
Digital print / 42 x 59.5cm / Collection: The artist

Myora fern 1985, printed 1987
Gelatin silver photograph / 17.8 x 22.6cm (comp.) / Purchased 1987 / Collection: Queensland Art Gallery / p.42

Opening of the Performing Arts Centre 1985, printed 2013*
Digital print / 42 x 59.5cm

Sand mining, Stradbroke Island 1985, printed 2013
Digital print / 42 x 59.5cm / Collection: The artist

Billabong Creek, Jerilderie 1986, printed 1987
Gelatin silver photograph / 40.8 x 31.6cm (comp.) / Purchased 1987 / Collection: Queensland Art Gallery / p.4

Swamp, Amity 1986, printed 1987
Gelatin silver photograph / 17.7 x 22.6cm (comp.) / Purchased 1987 / Collection: Queensland Art Gallery / pp.2–3

The apotheosis of Scott Redford 1987, printed 2013
Digital print / 59.5 x 42cm / Collection: The artist / p.55

Christopher Cook, organist 1987, printed 2013
Digital print / 59.5 x 42cm / Collection: The artist

Timber fret panel, Bundaberg 1987, printed 2013*
Digital print / 42 x 59.5cm / p.45

Expo 88 forest 1988, printed 2013*
Digital print / 59.5 x 42cm

Luke Roberts, Bellas Gallery 1988, printed 2013*
Digital print / 42 x 59.5cm / p.54

Reflections, Central Plaza, Brisbane 1988, printed 2013
Digital print / 59.5 x 42cm / Collection: The artist

View of Brisbane, bicentenary year 1988, printed 2013
Digital print / 84.1 x 118.9cm / Collection: The artist / pp.62–3

Final call of the dredge 'Brisbane' 1989, printed 2013
Digital print / 59.5 x 42cm / Collection: The artist / p.41

Melaleuca and reeds, Myora 1989, printed 2013
Digital print / 218.8 x 111.8cm / Collection: The artist / p.35

Door to the bath house, Rhondda Colliery 1990, printed 2013*
Digital print / 42 x 59.5cm / p.19

Mona Ryder 1990, printed 2013
Digital print / 59.5 x 42cm / Collection: The artist / p.52

Stair hall, house at Mermaid Beach 1990, printed 2013*
Digital print / 42 x 59.5cm / p.59

Casting boxes, Rylance Brickworks 1991, printed 2013
Digital print / 59.5 x 42cm / Collection: The artist / p.48

Emily Kame Kngwarreye in her studio 1991, printed 2013*
Digital print / 59.5 x 42cm / p.21

Interior, Boggo Road Gaol 1992, printed 2013*
Digital print / 59.5 x 42cm / p.47

Corinthian capitals, Brisbane City Hall 1998, printed 2013
Digital print / 42 x 59.5cm / Collection: The artist

Graffiti wall, Fortitude Valley 1998, printed 2013
Digital print / 59.5 x 42cm / Collection: The artist

Anne Wallace 2004, printed 2013*
Digital print / 59.5 x 42cm / p.53

Camel Head Rocks 2007, printed 2013
Digital print / 42 x 29.7cm / Collection: The artist

Fading rocks 2007, printed 2013
Digital print / 42 x 29.7cm / Collection: The artist

A mass of pandanus roots 2010, printed 2013
Digital print / 208.8 x 111.8cm / Collection: The artist

Melaleuca on the dune, Home Beach 2010, printed 2013
Digital print / 42 x 29.7cm / Collection: The artist

Pathway at Bumiera 2010, printed 2013
Digital print / 84.1 x 118.9cm / Collection: The artist

Photo tango, Deadman's Beach 2011, printed 2013
Digital print / 59.5 x 42cm / Collection: The artist

Bay window on the Red House 2012, printed 2013
Digital print / 42 x 29.7cm / Collection: The artist

Boswell's Court, Edinburgh 2012, printed 2013
Digital print / 42 x 29.7cm / Collection: The artist

Dining room in Alesund 2012, printed 2013
Digital print / 42 x 29.7cm / Collection: The artist

Summer in the North Sea 2012, printed 2013
Digital print / 29.7 x 42cm / Collection: The artist

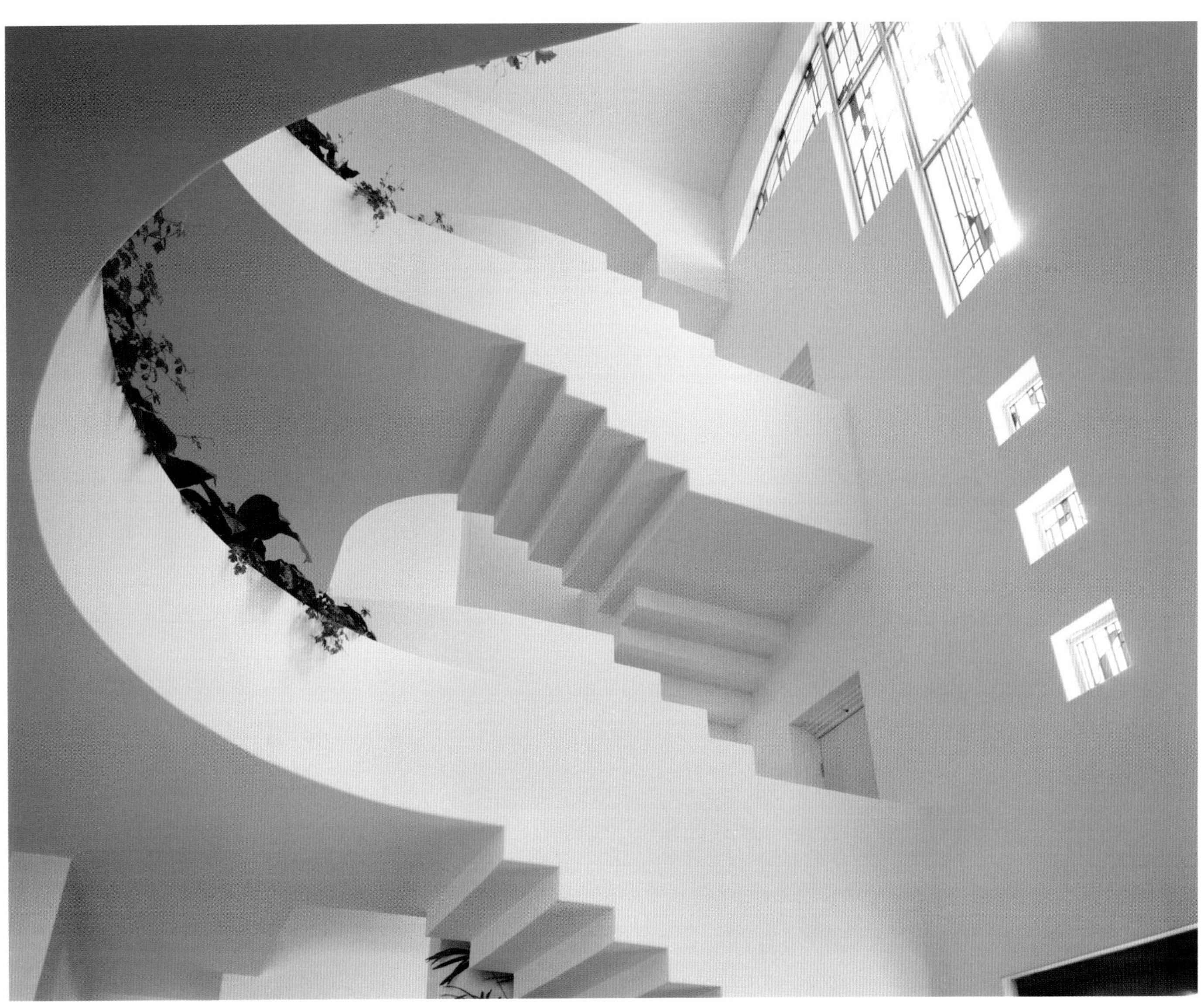

Stair hall, house at Mermaid Beach 1990, printed 2013

ACKNOWLEDGMENTS

SPONSORED BY
Glencore Xstrata

LENDERS
The Queensland Art Gallery | Gallery of Modern Art wishes to thank Richard Stringer for generously making available works from his own collection.

PROJECT SUPPORT
The Gallery thanks all those involved in the project, particularly Richard Stringer and Marguerite Stringer, for their cooperation and generosity in supporting the exhibition and accompanying publication.

The Gallery also extends its thanks to the following who provided invaluable and generous assistance for the project:
Stewart Armstrong, Executive Officer, National Trust of Queensland
Brisbane Digital Images, Milton
Christopher Hodges, Utopia Art Sydney
Peter Liddy

EXECUTIVE MANAGEMENT TEAM
Chris Saines, CNZM, Director
Celestine Doyle, Deputy Director, Marketing, Development and Commercial Services
Maud Page, Acting Deputy Director, Curatorial and Collection Development
Simon Wright, Assistant Director, Programming

CURATOR
Michael Hawker, Associate Curator, Australian Art

CURATORIAL SUPPORT
Julie Ewington, Curatorial Manager, Australian Art

PROJECT TEAM
Tarragh Cunningham, Exhibitions Manager
Teresa Morgan, Project Assistant
and staff

Tiffany Noyce, Acting Head of Registration
Desley Bischoff, Registrar, Exhibitions and Loans
Emma Schmeider, Registration Assistant, Exhibitions and Loans
and staff

Judy Gunning, Information and Publishing Services Manager
and staff

Bronwyn Klepp, Principal Marketing and Advertising Officer
Zoe Graham, Senior Sponsorship and Business Development Officer
Amelia Gundelach, Senior Media Officer
Sarah Stratton, Senior Communication Officer
and staff

Donna McColm, Head of Public Programs, Children's Art Centre and Membership
and staff

Michael O'Sullivan, Design Manager
Katrina Bell, Acting Senior Exhibition Designer
Jessica Stewart, Assistant Exhibition Designer
and staff

Amanda Pagliarino, Head of Conservation
Samantha Shellard, Conservator, Works on Paper
and staff

Dominique Jones, Acting Foundation Manager
and staff

PUBLICATION
Amy Moore, Graphic Designer
Rebecca Mutch, Editor
Art work photography: Natasha Harth, Photographer
Image assistance: Mark Sherwood, Assistant Photographer
Audiovisual coordination: Ben Wickes, Audio Visual Project Officer
Research assistance provided by the Queensland Art Gallery Research Library.

ARTIST ACKNOWLEDGMENTS
I wish to acknowledge the support from numerous people who Marguerite and I have met over the years and with whom we have been associated. This list is by no means exhaustive and there are many people who cannot be specifically acknowledged.

That said, in particular, I wish to thank:
Fred Hunt and the Fine Mono Photographic Group, Sue and John Railton, David and Patty Roessler, Howard and Mary Tanner, Don Watson and Judith McKay, my parents who supported me through thick and thin, my brother John, Sybil Curtis, Pullar family, Michael Snelling, Professor Ray Whitmore, Rita Avdiev, Miklos and Lynette Szilagyi, Dianne Byrne, Bettina and Desmond MacAulay, Glenn Cooke, Janet Hogan, Ray Fulton, Robin Gibson, Lindsay and Kerry Clare, our son Toby and wife Kate, our daughter Emma and husband Tom, Geoff Rae, and those who have facilitated access to properties, as well as the many staff of the Institute of Modern Art, National Trust of Queensland, Ipswich Art Gallery, State Library of Queensland and Queensland Art Gallery.

PUBLISHER
Queensland Art Gallery | Gallery of Modern Art
Stanley Place, South Bank, Brisbane
PO Box 3686, South Brisbane
Queensland 4101 Australia
www.qagoma.qld.gov.au

Published for 'Pleasure of Place: Photographs by Richard Stringer', an exhibition organised by the Queensland Art Gallery | Gallery of Modern Art (QAGOMA) and held at QAG, Brisbane, Australia, 26 October 2013 – 16 March 2014.

Curator: Michael Hawker, Associate Curator, Australian Art

National Library of Australia
Cataloguing-in-Publication entry
Author: Stringer, Richard, 1936- author.
Title: Pleasure of Place / photographs by Richard Stringer ; Michael Hawker.
ISBN: 9781921503573 (paperback)
Notes: Includes bibliographical references.
Subjects: Stringer, Richard, 1936---Exhibitions.
Architectural photography--Exhibitions.
Photography--Australia--Exhibitions.
Architecture in art--Exhibitions.
Other Authors/Contributors:
Hawker, Michael, author.
Queensland Art Gallery, issuing body
Dewey Number: 779.409943

NOTES ON THE PUBLICATION
The correct protocols have been observed with respect to the reproduction of the portrait of Emily Kame Kngwarreye on page 21 of this publication.

Dimensions of works are given in centimetres (cm), height preceding width followed by depth. Descriptive and attributed titles are in parenthesis.

Care has been taken to ensure the reproductions match as closely as possible the digital files of the original works.

Typeset in Flama. Image colour adjustment by Colour Chiefs and printing by Platypus. Cover printed on Sirio Pearl from Spicers, insides on Silk Matt from BJ Ball.

WARNING
It is customary in many Indigenous communities not to mention the name or reproduce photographs of the deceased. All such mentions and photographs in this publication are with permission. However, care and discretion should be exercised in using this book within Indigenous communities.

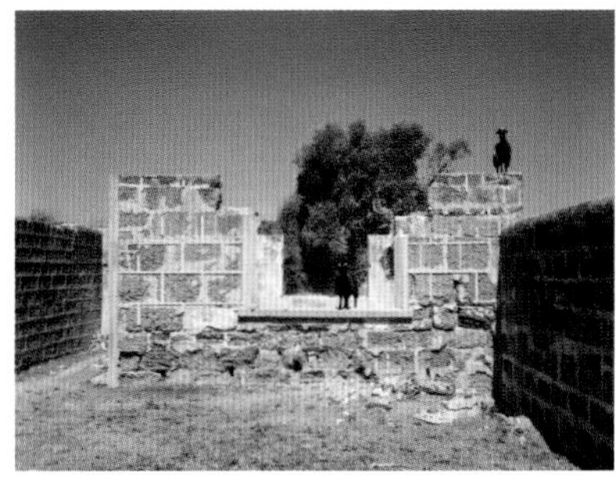

Cover: *Goats, St Helena Prison* 1977, printed 2013
Pages 2–3: *Swamp, Amity* (detail) 1986, printed 1987
Pages 62–3: *View of Brisbane, bicentenary year* (detail) 1988, printed 2013

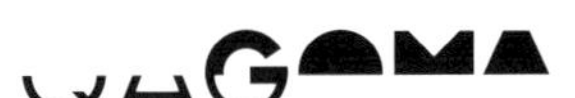
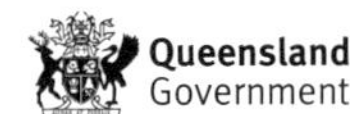

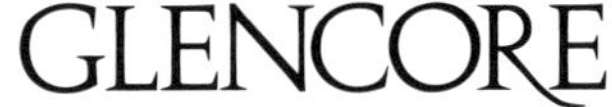

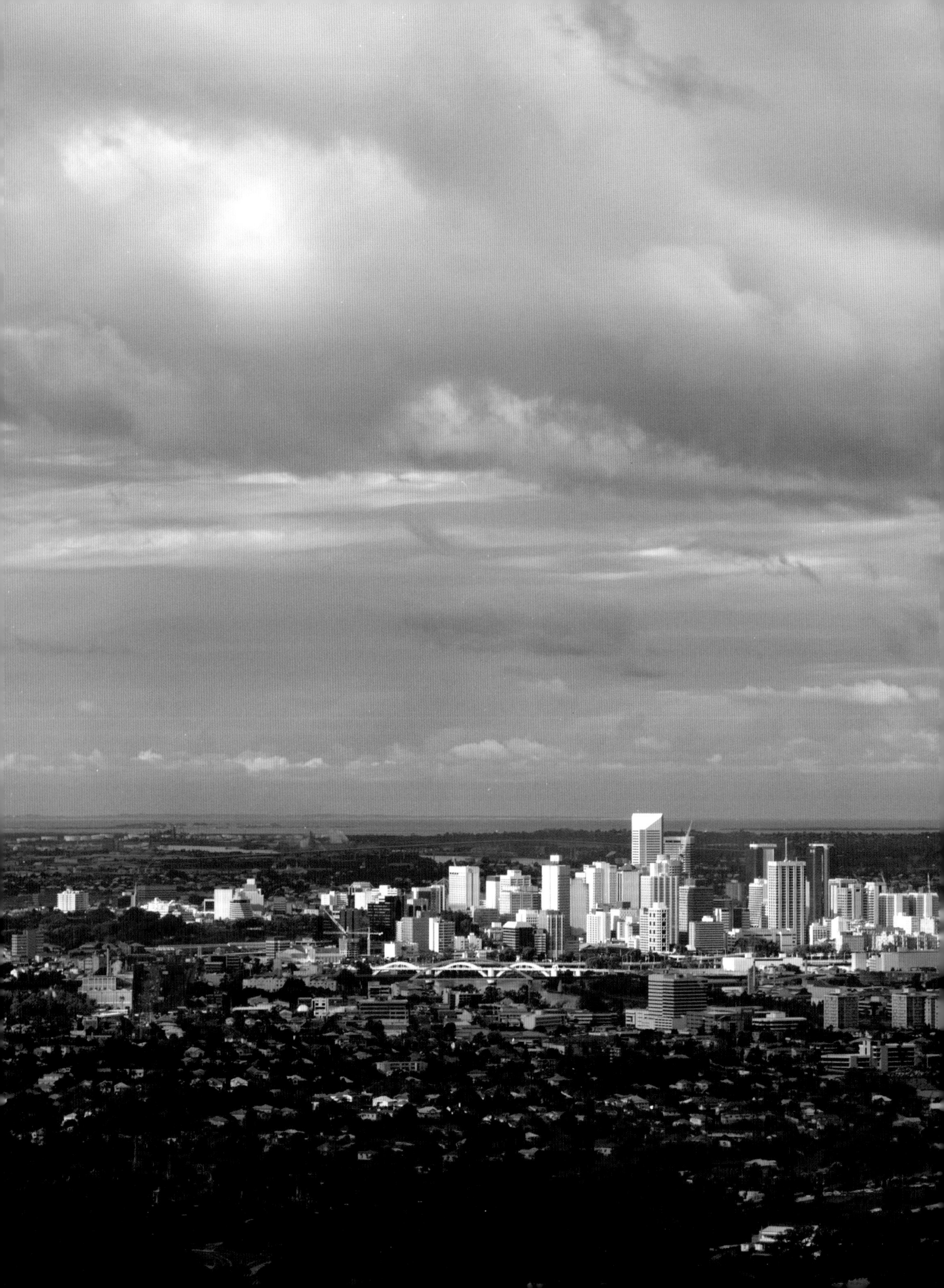

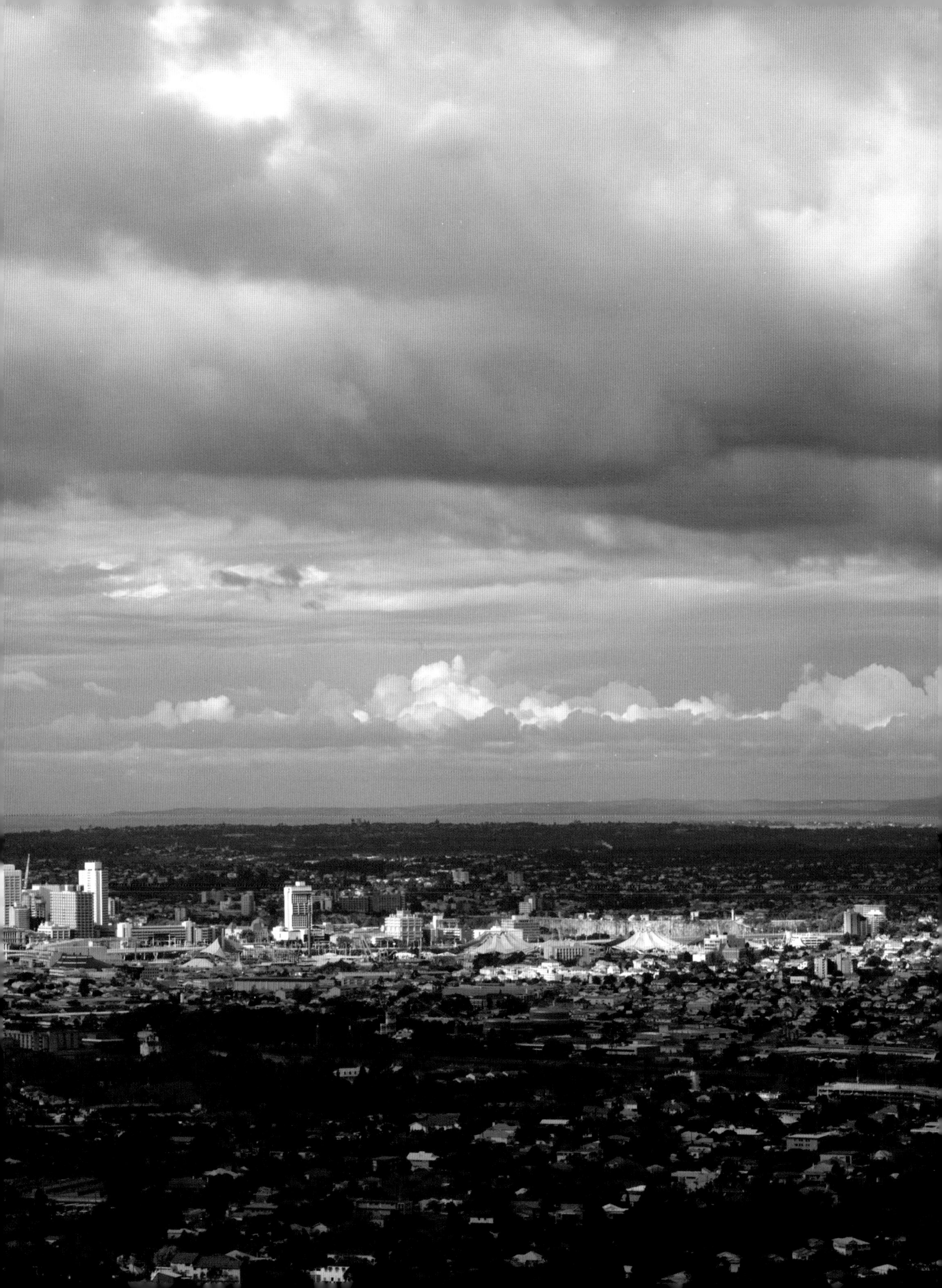